AFRICAN WOMEN CONNECT

HOW I STARTED AND GREW A NETWORKING GROUP OF AFRICAN IMMIGRANT WOMEN FOR FRIENDSHIP, BUSINESS, AND COMMUNITY.

Rita Jackson Apaloo

Published 2017.

For information,visit www.ritajapaloo.com.

Cover design by Ogunlade Tobi Samuel
Editing and formatting by Meagan Nicole

ISBN: 978-0-9988661-1-6

10 9 8 7 6 5 4 3 2 1

This book is dedicated to my husband Jacques and my kids Rae Simone, Jacques-Philippe, and Alice. I am grateful for your unending patience, interest and support of whatever's the object of my infinite desires. Your confidence in my ability to eventually "figure something out" motivates me even more! I love us!
Thank you!

Contents

Acknowledgements 7

Introduction..11

Suggestions on How to Use This Book...15

Preface..17

Chapter 1: The Power of Ongoing and Consistent Communication.....24

Chapter 2: Keeping Promises to Build Trust 31

Chapter 3: Using Feedback to Improve and Grow....................................39

Chapter 4: Planning the Work and Working the Plan 45

Chapter 5: Using Positivity to Combat Negativity 49

Chapter 6: Being Open to the Possibilities..55

Chapter 7: Being Kind, Welcoming, and Friendly....................................59

Chapter 8: Being Inclusive...63

Chapter 9: Keeping Time—Not African Time 67

Chapter 10: Providing Opportunities for Personal Growth....................73

Chapter 11: Not Taking Things Personally 79

Chapter 12: Being Creative and Innovative...85

Chapter 13: Being Brave and Bold..91

Chapter 14: Making It Relevant...97

Chapter 15: Being Engaging and Interactive..101

Chapter 16: Providing Food That Matters 107

Chapter 17: Monitoring and Evaluating Activities 113

Chapter 18: Reaching Out for Support 119

Chapter 19: Reflecting and Finding Meaning...........................127

Chapter 20: Being Grateful 143

AWCUnedited Information...147

AWCPhoto Album 189

About the Author 198

Acknowledgements

"BEING FEARLESS ISN'T BEING 100% NOT FEARFUL, IT'S
BEING TERRIFIED BUT YOU JUMP ANYWAY..."
— *TAYLOR SWIFT*

All I've ever wanted to be was fearless but for most of my life I had thewrong idea of what it takes. I thought I had to know it all, be it all and have no fear, in order to achieve being fearless. I know better now and I do love not being 100 percent but diving in any way because I have a community of people who help make it possible. Without their help, I would not have published this book.

Every day when I wake up next to you, I thank my lucky stars, Jacques! Your risk-taking abilities scare me and inspire me all at the same time, and this pushes me to pay close attention. I love you for that and more. I am so grateful for the space and support you gave me throughout this project. You are the best listener when it counts!

My children, Rae Simone, Jacques-Philippe and Alice, you guys are the best! Your interests and questions throughout the AWC years as well as while writing this book brought me joy and laughter. Knowing that you are part of this experience gives me hope that someday you will look back on this and make meaning however you choose.

My mother, Nellie, has been my number one fan and has always had great expectations of me, which can sometimes be scary! You are the ultimate fearless person that I know and your kind words and reminders of my younger self have spurred me on more than you know.

My dear friend, Bukola Oriola, has been my guide throughout this process. Your experience of having been down this road of authorship twice before, helped me avoid pitfalls that I may not have avoided otherwise. You held my hand throughout my self-publishing journey, and for that I will always be grateful.

To my team from the virtual self-publishing world, Meagan my copy editor and Samuel my book cover designer, your expertise and willingness to work with strangers to help them achieve their goals and dreams is amazing! I certainly couldn't have achieved this feat without your help. Thank you.

Finally, to my social media family, former AWC participants, family members and friends, I appreciate all your support and cheering on. I had no idea what to expect once I announced that I was working on this book. All you gave was encouragement and kindness. It made a huge difference in the process. Thank you!

It takes a village! You all are definitely my village because you make up whatever percentage I'm lacking to get to 100 percent!

Here's to being fearless!

DEAR READER

Thank you for your interest in African Women Connect: How I started and grew a networking group of African immigrant women for friendship, business, and community! I do hope you will find a few nuggets and be inspired to use them to make a difference however it applies to your personal situation.

African Women Connect (AWC) was created for African immigrant women to come together, get to know one another, build valuable relationships, share experiences and resources, and find solutions to issues affecting their community and them.

What made this group different than most like it was the fact that it reached beyond the usual one community, one country boundary. It is most comfortable to work with people from one's own country, but it's more enriching to get to know others and put ideas together by drawing on everyone's experiences to achieve common goals.

AWC embraced all women of African descent and aimed to promote valuable partnerships among all African immigrant women living abroad in the Minnesota Twin Cities area. The reason I chose to keep the focus on abroad living is because Africans are passionate about our home countries and personally connected to our people's needs and the challenges they face. However, as a group of women from many different countries, it would be almost impossible to decide to support one or a couple of causes without leaving many of our sisters disappointed. To ensure that we kept things neutral and to avoid disagreements, I encouraged women to get involved with other community organizations that focused on charitable causes supporting specific African communities that matched their interests.

Minnesota has a vibrant African immigrant population. According to the 2010 US Census statistics, over seventy-three thousand African-born immigrants live in Minnesota with over 60 percent from eastern Africa, about 25 percent from western African, and the remaining 15 percent from elsewhere in Africa. A majority of them live in the Twin Cities metro area, so I thought for sure I could find a few people to convince to join me in my quest. And find them I did.

During the more than six years of AWC's existence, its participants included women from the Bahamas, Benin, Burundi, Cameroon, Côte d'Ivoire, Eritrea, Ethiopia, Guyana, Ghana, Kenya, Liberia, Madagascar, Mali, Nigeria, Rwanda,

Senegal, Sierra Leone, Somalia, South Africa, Tanzania, Togo, United States, Zambia, and Zimbabwe.

Group meetings and events were organized to support different community initiatives,and specific topics including health and wellness, finance, entertainment, business, leadership, etc.

AWC's participants were very passionate about its purpose and strongly believed that such an organization was long overdue. Some incredible women joined AWC and were curious, excited, and interested enough to be a part of building a meaningful coalition of African women.

Always put in the category of black women in America, not much information about African women could be found to assist with planning and analysis prior to starting the group. While black women in America face similar challenges, African women's experiences are different from those of African-American women. One hope was to discover the unique attributes and circumstances of African women living in Minnesota and help to provide awareness and education to African communities and the larger community.

Each AWC participant played a role in helping to discover how we connected as African women and, therefore, contributed greatly in the creation of this book. My hope is that this book will be a great help to all as we continue on our lifelong journey of personal connections and our desire tohelp others make purposeful connections.

With gratitude,

Rita Jackson Apaloo

Suggestions on How to Use This Book

- Read from front cover to back cover.
- Skip around to chapters and sections that interest you the most.
- Read it through and then use it as a reference book for making personal connections or to help others connect.
- Contribute to the online conversation at www.ritajapaloo.com while you read or after you have read the book.
- Encourage other people to use this in your book club and then share your thoughts online at www.ritajapaloo.com.
- Share this book with others by gifting them with a copy or passing on your copy.
- Do something creative that is not on this list.

GETTING STARTED

At the very beginning, I had my mind set on starting a newsletter that featured African women and the things that they cared about. I believed there was a lot of stereotyping of African immigrant women and hardly any sources available to learn about the lives and dreams of African women. And even when Africans themselves talked about their experiences and needs, it was in silos from the perspective of specific communities (Liberian, Nigerian, Kenyan, etc.) or groups.

At the time, I felt like a hardcopy newsletter, distributed similarly to the local African newspapers already providing information to African immigrant communities, was ideal. I approached a couple of them to pitch a column, but they weren't ready to give away an inch of their space to an unknown woman who was not even a journalist from back home. They were doing serious news of what was happening in Africa, the United States, and the local community and providing information and resources people in the community needed and depended on. As far as they were concerned, what I proposed was mostly opinion and entertainment and gossip. So, it didn't fly.

After considering the responses that I was getting, I decided to give it a shot on my own and figure out a way to deliver my message to my primary audience—African women. One thought was to have my newsletter as an insert in a newspaper and another idea was to produce an e-magazine on the internet, which was starting to take hold at the time as more people gained computer access through their work, school, library, and home.

After attempting to write a couple of short articles, I wasn't pleased with my results. I wanted to write things that were current, important, and relatable to African women and their families living in the United States, and specifically in Minnesota where I lived.

Once I started thinking about this dream more and more and talking to people around me, especially my husband, I felt that the answer came to me clearly—find a way to get to know African women better.

As a young, single, and independent female living and working in the United States, I spent a lot of time going to parties and events and meeting people of similar age, both females and males. I formed really good friendships with other young African females, and we enjoyed getting together and talking about our lives and our dreams. I especially enjoyed meeting others from different African countries and learning more about them and how we a similar or different in our upbringing, beliefs, values, and worldviews. In the United States, all Africans are often seen as one community, but Africans know that we are as diverse as our continent of fifty-four countries. We make up a plethora of ethnic groups, cultures, languages, and more.

Fascinatingly, as I became friends with more Africans outside of my Liberian immigrant community, I quickly realized a pattern. Although I enjoyed spending time with my new African friends, at the end of the day, they always saw me as the "Liberian friend." Our friendship was somewhat surfaced and never got deeper due to all kinds of stereotypes, myths, and perceptions. In other words, we could laugh and talk about was happening on our jobs, at our children's schools, or the struggles of living in the United States, but we could not talk about what we were experiencing collectively as a single immigrant community.

This idea that we come from different places and, therefore, couldn't be really good friends is ingrained in many people. We were not making the connection that we had overarching desires and challenges. We may experience them differently as individual communities, but at the end of the day, we all want the same thing—a better life in America for ourselves and our children. We could work together to achieve that on a great level as individuals, as country-based African communities, and as a collective African immigrant community. I knew that

Rita Jackson Apaloo

attempting to bring about this kind of change was almost impossible (as I was warned numerous times). However, I wanted to try.

The more I studied the situation, the more I was convinced that the only way I could write pieces that would be interesting and relevant to African women and their families was for me to get to know them on a deeper level. I thought that I could do that in two ways: interviewing people for the newsletter and social gatherings where I could provide opportunities for women to connect with each other, learn, share, discover, and have fun. So, I set out to do just that.

I came up with a plan to start the newsletter, and I tweaked things a bit to guide my new idea of getting African women together. I first needed a name for the group and a compelling reason why people should join. The name Women from Africa Connect (WFAC) was my first try. I thought it said exactly who and what but just didn't flow well. In addition, I wanted the acronyms to easily be sounded out so WFAC did not meet that criteria, which sent me back to the drawing board.

I liked African Women Connect (AWC) better. It was concise, easy to sound out the acronyms, and had the magic three words and letters, which made it easy to remember as well.

Getting to the right mission statement took a lot more heads than just mine. After AWC's first gathering, I took advantage of the excitement and asked for input in creating the mission and vision statements. I convinced my sisters, a couple of friends, and their close friends to help craft the mission and vision of AWC. The small group of women, providing me with much needed input and support, agreed that the word "empower" should be included in the mission statement, and after some urging from me, they also agreed that participants should benefit first as individuals and then secondly as group or community.

I am very pleased with the final mission and vision statements we collaborated on, and to this day, I am still proud of it and the input and buy in from other women who were beneficiaries of the work of AWC. Those words are just as powerful today as they were on that winter day in 2004.

Over the years, the statements have stayed the same, but they have been expressed in several ways in different communication pieces that conveyed the same original idea— coming together to benefit both the individual and the community.

AWC Mission Statement

The mission of AWC is to create a network to empower women of African descent, linking them to valuable resources and promoting partnerships that strengthen individual and communal success.

AWC Vision Statement

We envision a world where African women are viewed and recognized as valuable contributors to society by themselves and others.

The AWC Movement

AWC is more than a social gathering to have fun and get together with old and new friends. It's a movement to connect African women to find their collective voice and build a stronger community.

The Purpose of AWC

The main purpose of this group is for African immigrant women to come together, get to know one another, build valuable relationships, share experiences and resources, and find solutions to issues affecting us and our community.

Branding AWC

In addition to naming the organization and creating mission and vision statements, having a logo was a way to create a visual and name recognition in a way that resonated with the audience—African women. The first logo was handmade by me. This was mostly due to limited resources, skills, and funds. It was also because I needed something fairly quickly, and the best way I knew how to get things done quickly and to my specification was to do it myself. That would definitely not work well if a leader was looking for buy in from key stakeholders, but that was not the case for AWC. So, I had the autonomy.

I drew it by hand and then created a silhouette of it for a different effect. The entire creation from beginning to review took me a couple of days. Once I got to a point where I was happy with the results, I asked past AWC event participants to vote on their favorite one and tell me what they liked or disliked about each drawing and why. In the end, I combined elements from both, and that is how the first official AWC logo was created.

A couple of years later, I wanted a more polished look, so I hired a graphic designer to create the current logo. The process was very different from the first one, as you can imagine. It took a lot of back and forth in order to get it to where I was satisfied. At one point, there were up to four silhouettes of women's heads, which was paired down to two, one with a head wrap and the other natural-looking. It was also important to me that the word "connect" was emphasized. The logo was finalized while sitting in front of a laptop in a small African restaurant in Minneapolis. It made all the difference working out the final kinks together in person with the graphic designer. I am very proud of the final design. However, the change did not go unnoticed by participants who fell in love with the first logo, but they accepted the transition eventually.

Chapter 1

THE POWER OF ONGOING AND CONSISTENT COMMUNICATION

C ommunication is the most powerful way a person can connect to another person. Communication is defined as a means of transmitting information from one person or place to another. There is always at least one sender and one receiver.

Research shows that although it sounds quite simple, communication is by no means easy because there are a lot of opportunities for errors to occur when sending and receiving messages. Errors may include a poorly crafted message, the use of the wrong channel or media to send the message, or a receiver who gets the message in a way that the sender did not intend. It takes a lot for communication to be transmitted effectively and successfully to a specific audience—research, knowledge, skills, and experience are required. In addition, the message would have to reach the audience in a timely manner, and they would have to interpret it as intended and be moved to act in a way that the sender hoped.

There are many challenges of effective communication between two people or entities, and those challenges are only compounded in the case of mass communication — be it dozens, hundreds, or more — which includes multiple elements and levels. On this level, errors don't only multiply but also become costly both socially and financially.

I appreciate good communication from individuals and organizations, so when it came to AWC, I let my personal experience guide my efforts. It gave me some comfort that my audience was made up of women like myself who shared similar experiences.

For example, my "over communicate" strategy can be credited to the fact that I prefer to be "in the know." I would rather receive too much information than too little or none at all. During times when I felt like I didn't have enough information to be involved, I ended up withdrawing and losing interest. My personal preference motivated me to keep communication lines open and flowing constantly for AWC.

The strategy was to mix up AWC communication in terms of types and channels so that it didn't sound boring or redundant. Below is a list of the different forms of communication I used for AWC.

Website: This served as an online brochure with information about AWC and links to other online sites like the blog and Meetup sites. The website allowed AWC to be searchable online, and it was a way for women to contact us via email, social media or telephone.

Calendar of Events: Our Google calendar hosted event information, which was determined early in the year. The calendar was uploaded to the website for all to access. Event information was also submitted to community newspapers to be added to calendar of events listings.

Telephone Calls: Telephone numbers were captured at events through sign-in and sign-up forms. They were used to call people a couple of days before each event, especially people who were not responding to email messages. It was also noted when a person preferred a phone call rather than an email to ensure that we honored their primary contact preference.

Email: Email was our primary form of contact. People who were interested in AWC got an email about how they could contact us and also letting them know that they were being added to our LISTSERV®. New participants received a welcome email, including upcoming events and opportunities to get involved. All event attendees received a brief thank you message twenty-four to forty-eight hours after the event, and everyone on the LISTSERV® received a summary of the event no later than a week after. This summary came in the form of an email with links to our blog and website, and it included pictures of the event and the date of the next event.

Regular Mail: Mailing was used sparingly due mainly to the cost. Thank you letters to partner organizations, greeting cards, and hard copy newsletters (which were discontinued after a couple of mailings) were things sent by regular mail.

E-newsletter: Due to the cost of postage, I switched to an e-newsletter using an email marketing program that charged a monthly fee. Sent periodically, the AWC e-newsletter highlighted past events, partnerships, insights, survey results, profiles, and links of interest to our audience.

Logo: Our logo is a symbol of the organization that conveyed a message of who we are using images and words.

Blog: Our blog included stories of AWC events, images, news, and stories that reinforced messages and ideas supported by AWC.

Social Media: Social media tools were used mainly for event management purposes. Evite™ is a free event management program that allowed me to create and send invitations to participants. I could also track RSVPs, send personal and group messages, provide location address and maps, and send reminders as often as I needed to the entire list or a segment of the list.

Meetup is a social media site that was used to create an AWC group. Meetup brings thousands of people with similar interests together in cities to form relationships and do more together. For a monthly fee, AWC was registered as a Meetup in Minnesota to increase awareness and widen the net to reach more African women in the area.

AWC groups were also created on Facebook, Linked-In, and Twitter for the purpose of keeping people connected outside of AWC events so that they could continue to build meaningful relationships.

Publications: Brochures, business cards, flyers, annual reports, promotional and educational handouts, etc., were created and used as needed.

Word of Mouth: This form of communication was critical in spreading the word about AWC. To this day, African communities continue to rely heavily on those they know and trust, more than commercials and marketing campaigns. Participants who were excited about their AWC experiences were happy to share with others, and they motivated others to check AWC out. Equally so, those who did not have positive experiences were also eager to share with others—it worked both ways.

Tabling/Community Events/Fairs: Tabling at community events made it possible to get out in the communities and meet people, share our purpose and story, make connections, build relationships, and gather information to increase our mailing list and number of participants.

Publicity: Featured articles, news stories, interviews, panel participation, contributing articles, and news releases were other ways AWC's work was communicated.

AWC Social Events: Ongoing gatherings were another way to provide information and promote all things AWC— upcoming programs and events, the various channels of communication, social interaction with like-minded people, capture experiences through pictures to promote AWC and its ideas, get feedback to improve, and capture event information.

Communication tools available today that would have benefited AWC are things like text messaging, video messaging, live video streaming, and a variety of apps used to connect, form, and manage groups.

With AWC's communication mix, it was difficult to miss keeping in the loop no matter if the person missed one or several events. People had multiple ways of accessing information through several different communication channels. As a result, participants always felt connected and in the know about AWC, which resulted in a sense of belonging to the group. It was like getting right back to where they left off without feeling like they'd lost touch or needed someone to catch them up.

Another benefit of the mix was the time- and cost-saving aspects. Many of the tools and programs required a lengthy set up that usually included entering data and general information, but once the initial set up was done, it saved a lot of time and provided a lot of benefits. In addition, the tools allowed AWC to build relationships with the individuals over the long-term once their information was stored in the appropriate data files or accounts.

AWC's communication mix may seem like a lot, but it was done tastefully with strategy and understanding of the audience. I don't remember getting feedback that indicated people were feeling overwhelmed by the information or the frequency of the communication they received. I believe that providing quality, effective, and constant communication led to success in building relationships with so many women over a long period of time.

Chapter 2

KEEPING PROMISES TO BUILD TRUST

K eeping a promise is as simple as making a commitment and following through with it. Following through on a promise shows that some thought was put into the decision or action in order to make it happen and demonstrates a high level of respect and relevance for the person on the other end of that promise.

I regarded AWC's mission, vision, tagline, goals, and objectives as part of a larger organizational promise and commitment to participants. I referred to them to guide me in developing my long-term and short-term strategic goals, annual activities, and personal promises I made in my interactions with participants.

One definition of a mission statement is an overarching, timeless expression of your purpose and aspiration, addressing both what you seek to accomplish and the manner in which you seek to accomplish it. I see the mission statement as a declaration of why my organization exists. So it would be confusing, at least to me, if an organization were found to be engaged in activities that are completely different from what their mission claims.

For example, the mission of AWC is to create a network to empower women of African descent, linking them to valuable resources and promoting partnerships that strengthen individual and communal success. I was intentional about ensuring that all of my efforts aligned with this promise.

Imagine if a person had come to our event and found themselves in the midst of a group of women from Minnesota's North Country dressed in African attire and having interesting conversations about the state of family farms back home. Or consider this scenario: On a woman's first visit to an AWC event, there are only three other attendees present, but she hears about great possibilities of a larger and more diverse group of women. She returns the second time only to meet the same three attendees she had met before. The woman, being somewhat of an optimist, decides to give it one last chancebut disappointingly,she meets the exact same three attendees from the two events before. These examples may sound extreme, but when we make promises and don't fulfill them, the results can feel just as extreme.

It was important to me that the women who took the time to get involved in AWC felt that our events and activities were not a result of afterthought. I wanted to show them that AWC events were intentionally planned actions that aligned with our promises and created both personal and collective value for them.

Too often I see organizations create impressive missions, visions, goals, and objectives, but their activities do not match up with their promises. I've observed situations where groups do whatever is trending in the community. For example, a social group that aims to provide fun activities and opportunities to support group members in various life situations decides to ship barrels of household and personal items to people in Africa. It sounds like a noble and good cause, but it can easily get out of hand when you consider finding the items and then the cost of shipping. How does that project align with their group founding goals? Letting your original goals and objectives guide your actions and activities is a great way to keep your promises to your audience.

Before making any promises, it is important to think things through, understand what you're committing yourself or organization to, and ensure that it makes sense in terms of what you're trying to accomplish. Make sure your goals are SMART (Specific, Measurable, Actionable, Realistic, and Time-related). I enjoy using the SMART goals strategy because it is easy to be accountable if the steps are followed. Also, keep in mind that in order to fulfill promises, you must consider your time, talent, money, and means.

Another thing that helped me keep my promises was to put them in writing. This way you and others can point to the promise and easily determine whether or not the action was taken. I am a person who respects the written word, so all of AWC's promises were written in multiple places for the general public to access. Written information was shared multiple times in various publications and through a variety of communication channels as I mentioned in Chapter 1.

AWC activities and events were often scheduled during an annual strategic planning phase, which was prior to the year-end. I made sure to stick with dates and times as indicated on the schedule. Finding and booking venues were not as easy to plan so far in advance, but it was done weeks in advance. This allowed participants enough time to do any research and coordination needed to plan their attendance. Various checklists and agendas helped to guide us through on our promises. Having a checklist made it easier to communicate the plan, share with volunteers, ask for any additional support, and keep track of what was needed to be done on a daily, weekly, monthly, and yearly basis.

There were times when AWC event dates were in conflict with bigger community-specific events. People in African immigrant communities know of this unwritten rule that if an individual or group has a big community-specific event planned (like an Independence Day program that draws a large crowd), members of that community are expected to steer clear of that date or risk some type of retaliation. There's a lot of pressure on event participants because at the end of day, it is all about loyalty—to whom are you more loyal?

This is a typical "brownie points" situation where a person could gain favor or put a relationship in jeopardy depending on their choice of event. For example, if I invite you to my milestone birthday bash and you decide to attend a community group gala ball instead, you should be ready to look me in the face and explain why you chose them over me. And if I'm not happy with your reasoning, it could hurt our relationship badly or sever it for good. This is serious community business that could determine success or failure of an event.

Because I am Liberian, there was a large number of women from the Liberian community who participated in AWC. Whenever a big event was happening in the Liberian community on the same day as an AWC event, I expected that most, if not all, of AWC's regular participants who were Liberian to be no shows at the AWC event. There were times when people suggested that I cancel AWC scheduled events in honor of the larger community event that they saw as more important. My answer was always "no" because I had to keep my promise and stick to the AWC plan.

Although I knew that AWC attendance would likely be lower than usual due to the bigger event, it was critical that the event went on as planned because there were women from other communities who wanted to attend. AWC's doors were always open for that one woman who made it there. More importantly, I always made certain that it was a great event and experience with nothing spared. Keeping the promise for one woman was just as important as keeping the promise for a roomful of women.

Turning down suggestions to cancel events to adhere to community unwritten rules was uncomfortable. I lost a few people as the result, especially in cases where the individuals regarded their AWC participation as a personal favor to our friendship or their friendship with another AWC participant and not because they regarded the experience as a valuable use of their time. It was disappointing on one hand, but on the other, it was relieving. My aim was always to connect people who saw value in the mission and vision of AWC for themselves and for the collective community of African women.

Did I ever break a promise? Yes, I did. Even with all the strategies in place to ensure I followed through on AWC's promises, sometimes things were beyond my control. When promises were broken, I communicated transparently and early with the appropriate information—apology, what went wrong, how it was going to be fixed, or what the next steps were.

One example of a broken promise was when we planned to have a Mother's Day event but due to low interest, it had to be cancelled. The idea was to have a small and informal event that provided the opportunity for women to be celebrated by their significant others and families. I quickly realized that people had traditions and rituals for celebrating Mother's Day, and they were not willing to make any changes. In addition, I couldn't seem to get the event fee right in order to cover the event costs. I also learned that not many people celebrated outside of an elaborate church program. Those were enough reasons to cancel the event and chart the experience as "lesson learned."

I took the role of ensuring I kept the promises of AWC to each and every AWC participant seriously. I created goals and actions that matched what we promised using the SMART goals strategy. When a commitment could not be fulfilled, it was communicated openly and honestly and in a solution-driven way with a focus on building lasting relationships. Winning participants' trust was optimal in the success of AWC meeting its mission, vision, goals, and objectives.

Chapter 3

USING FEEDBACK TO IMPROVE AND GROW

I believe that communication is the miracle ingredient for success in many aspects of life and business, butone-way communication can be detrimental to communication efforts. It is not much fun being the only one doing the talking, neither is it fun to be the one being talked to without acknowledgement or the opportunity to provide feedback.

Feedback was critical in checking the pulse of AWC participants, and providing them with the opportunity to give input to create an organization relevant to them brought value to them and the organization. Two-way communication has tremendous benefits and advantages when it comes to building relationships, but it is not without its challenges.

One advantage of intentionally providing two-way communication was increased engagement. When participants were asked to respond to surveys or provide information, they received a follow up directly related to their response. In addition, it was clear what the follow up information was connected to, why it was important, and what the next steps were.

One example of how two-way communication increased engagement was with our sign-in sheets at each event. Participants were encouraged to sign in at every meeting. There was always a nicely formatted sign-in sheet for people to write in their names, mailing address, telephone number, and email address. There was also a "notes" column to include reminders or make any special requests. I made a fuss about the sign-in sheet because the information was used to write a blog post about the event for everyone to access. It was also used to track attendance at each event throughout the year, which was used in AWC's annual and historical reports that were shared with the participants and the public. In addition, the information was also used to make other analyses that resulted in various planning, execution, and evaluation of activities. Seeing the many ways the information they provided was used, participants were happy to play their part in helping grow and improve AWC.

Two-way communication helped to quickly analyze audience reactions whenever needed. Once information was released, I paid close attention to the responses I received. I listened, acknowledged feedback, and consider reactions, big and small, as I made decisions that affected people's AWC experience. This included what questions they asked, how they responded or passed the message on to others, and what actions they took, depending on how they interpreted the message. If it was clear that there was a breakdown in communication or a misunderstanding of a message, I could intervene and fix whatever had been misconstrued.

This strategy also empowered participants. They understood that their contributions and opinions were valued and necessary for AWC's success. Power-sharing in this way gave women the confidence to speak up about not only the bad but also the good of the organization.

Another gain from two-way communication was the opportunity to build trust and loyalty with participants like a friendship.When people first get to know each other,they are careful in their communication. As they get more comfortable with each other, they get bolder in their communication and aren't afraid to ask questions or make truthful comments. The longer I practiced and welcomed this form of communication, the more successful our communication became. It was not always smooth sailing, but sticking with it made it better. The number of mistakes became fewer as time went on, and my relationships became more meaningful both personally and collectively.

As I mentioned before, the decision to practice two-way communication and allow feedback was not without hurdles and challenges. It is always much easier to do things alone and be the one and final say than having to wait for others to respond, take their thoughts and ideas into consideration, and then negotiate a new solution or compromise. For one thing, the process is slower when you are looking to include others. Like the African proverb says, "If you want to go fast, go alone, but if you want to go far, go together." This proverb demonstrates both the challenges and benefits of two-way communication strategy.

The biggest challenge was sorting through the large volume of feedback. Determining which ones were valid and which ones were just people being disgruntle about any and everything could be tricky. The real question was which ones would impact AWC in a significant way, good or bad. And I definitely could not say yes to everyone and everything—that's just terrible leadership. What kept me focused was the fact that there was always a well-thought-out plan in place to guide me back on the path that I believed (with input from participants) was the best one for AWC. Those times when I was unsure how to react to a specific feedback, I went back to AWC's plan and determined whether or not it fit in our plan.

From the very beginning, feedback was requested around the mission and vision of the organization. I believed that in order for AWC to work, there had to be buy in from African women. Yes, I am an African woman, but there is a wide range of us. There was no way that I could speak on their behalf or speculate about what they needed and expected from AWC.

Requesting feedback was a constant and ongoing activity throughout the life of AWC, and it was done in a variety of formats, including one-on-one conversations, group discussions, event feedback forms, surveys, emails, and the website. Feedback was requested on everything from frequency of events, start and end times, event venues, topics and speakers, and most and least liked aspects of their experience at an AWC event, among other things. There were ample opportunities to provide verbal or written feedback, and ultimately, it led to important changes and improvements along the way.

Improvements to program delivery in terms of interest and relevancy to the key audience came from feedback activities. Some included group volunteer work in the community, providing a mix of social and professional growth opportunities, and suggestions on themes, topics, speakers, venues, potential participants and collaborations, etc.

Feedback completed the circle of AWC communication. Because it was an integral part of AWC, in many ways, it fueled the trajectory of the organization.

Two-way communication and gathering feedback was a great way to further AWC's mission, empower women, be transparent, and strengthen relationships and trust with the women.

Chapter 4

PLANNING THE WORK AND WORKING THE PLAN

A s the saying goes, one who fails to plan plans to fail. All organizations, big or small, formal or informal, need to plan if they expect to succeed. This is no different for individuals. I believe that planning is the lifeline to success. Without a plan, success will be sporadic, and it would be easier to stray unintentionally from reaching goals, objectives, and purpose.

From the onset of AWC, strategic planning was an essential part of the organization, and it was used as a way to set the stage for the work I intended to do. According to businessdictionary.com, strategic planning is described as follows:

A systematic process of envisioning a desired future, and translating this vision into broadly defined goals or objectives and a sequence of steps to achieve them.

In contrast to long-term planning (which begins with the current status and lays down a path to meet estimated future needs), strategic planning begins with the desired-end and works backward to the current status.

- *At every stage of long-range planning the planner asks, "What must be done here to reach the next (higher) stage?"*
- *At every stage of strategic-planning the planner asks, "What must be done at the previous (lower) stage to reach here?"*

Also, in contrast to tactical planning (which focuses at achieving narrowly defined interim objectives with predetermined means), strategic planning looks at the wider picture and is flexible in choice of its means.

AWC's initial business plan included the organization's mission, vision, goals, objectives, and all other standard elements of a business plan, but it was by no means perfect. I did not seek help as I should have, and I got stuck on the budget and financial analysis section of the plan. I was always a good student at mathematics, but I'm no financial analyst. I quickly found that financial analysis is very different than simply adding and subtracting.

In my eagerness to get on with the areas I was most excited about — strategies to connect women and help them expand their networks — I skipped the financial analysis portion. I later learned that financial analysis is the most important part of any business plan. Even though I convinced myself that I would revisit it at a later date once I got things off the ground, it never happened. I strongly believe that had I gotten help and worked through the financials, AWC's story would have ended much differently.

I created a basic, strategic plan for AWC, using a format I had learned about through my day job. It was a one-page strategic plan that included things like the mission, vision, objectives, strategies, and action plans. It worked well at the time and served as needed.

Subsequent long- and short-range plans I created focused on goals, objectives, and tactics needed to increase number of participants attending events, as well as repeat attendance of each attendee. My intent was to gradually move things along to where I wanted to end up—a membership organization. The social and personal development events were free in the beginning. Later, participants were expected to contribute a suggested amount to pay for food, and then it finally moved to a point where the event was free but attendees had to purchase their meal as a way to support the hosting business. Clearly, none of the above was enough to sustain an organization's basic operation. Administrative duties needed to plan and organize events were all done on my time and with the help of a volunteer or two from time to time.

A majority of the money and resources that sustained AWC came from my personal finances and time. The organization was my idea, my dream, and my passion. It was important to me to do everything I could to make it work. Even when it was clear that I needed to bring things to a halt, it was a struggle, but I had to consider my family, from whom I was taking money and a tremendous amount of time and energy, and decide what made sense. In the end, I had to face the fact that AWC was not generating enough money to support its day to day operations.

The more AWC grew in number of participants, the clearer it became that I needed to go back and develop a financial plan to support its growth. Once the basic math was done, I determined that it would take more than what the participants were willing to pay in order for it to be successful. Some people suggested that AWC become a nonprofit organization or a program of a nonprofit organization. However, that was never my dream, and I believed that it was not the appropriate format for what I had built so far.

Another challenge was the need for additional heads, hands, and hearts to move the organization forward. Even though we were able to bring a few people on board to assist with event planning, strategic planning was not something most people expected or wanted to be a part of. So, due to a lack of interest and a solid plan to move forward, AWC stalled.

Although flawed, AWC's strategic long- and short-range planning allowed me to continue to provide activities and events relevant to my key audience — African women. In addition, strategic planning also helped me to meet deadlines, set goals and objectives, and take the necessary action steps.

Chapter 5

USING POSITIVITY TO COMBAT NEGATIVITY

S uspicion, mistrust, and doubt are a few words that most Africans can relate to on some level. Sad to say, those words fit in nicely with African cultural beliefs and values around human nature, especially when it comes to working with African people. There are a few reasons that explain why, including historical factors around colonization and exploitation of African people and nations, poverty, corruption, greed, lack of education and resources, family and personal misfortune, voodoo/evil practices, etc.

Unfortunately, the ramifications of such cultural values and practices are not limited to personal relationships. They show up in groups and organizations run by individuals who ascribe to such beliefs and practices. I believe that most people do these things unconsciously because that is how they were raised, and it has become a way of survival for them. Dragging others down is a way that some Africans believe that they will be lifted up. This is sad but true.

Organizations are led and managed by humans. And if there's one thing we know for sure, humans are complicated. The culture and tone of an organization is set by its leadership. Usually, when the person in charge of an African-led organization is an African, other Africans are often suspicious of that leader and his or her work and objectives.

AWC was no exception to that rule. Right off the bat, there were a lot of questions about my country of origin, education, experience, family background, marital status, parental status, line of work, and the list goes on and on. People wanted to know the "real" story behind AWC's purpose. Not surprisingly, some suspected a hidden agenda and were determined to figure out what the hype was all about.

I discovered very quickly that there was always a long list of reasons that people could come up with to challenge me as a person or my capability to achieve what I promised. Being an African myself, I understood where all these misgivings were coming from—a history, culture, and values system that begins on the premise that a person will take advantage of others as long as they let them. I too had my struggles with suspicion and mistrust, so I understood where they were coming from. However, I have been intentional over the years to give people the benefit of the doubt. I'm not perfect, but I am determined to combat negativity with positivity, kindness, and hope.

More than once, I have been described as the type of person who is always "looking at the bright side of things," sometimes to my detriment. That attitude greatly influenced AWC's content and communication. I deliberately and intentionally designed my communication and interactions to be optimistic, upbeat, and forward-looking. Sometimes I had to write and rewrite information and messages several times to ensure they were just the right tone. Over time, it got easier and became almost second nature. In the end, optimism and positivity became part of AWC's branding and made a huge difference in outreach and retention efforts.

Giving people the benefit of the doubt was easier said than done though. I vividly remember when I had to be reminded to live what I preached. At one of our biggest events one year, I had a couple of volunteers help collect fees and run the program because I had to play the role of a host. At the end of the event, I was checking the money we had collected and noticed that there were a few checks in the bunch. When I came across a check with an unfamiliar name, I remembered saying something like, "Oh, boy, I hope it cashes without incident. I should have required people to pay in cash only, especially if they are not regular attendees." One of the volunteers responded, "Don't say that. You have to trust people. I'm sure she wouldn't give you a check that she knows isn't good. Give her the benefit of the doubt." That was a great lesson for me that night, and I appreciated it. She held me accountable to my own promise of positivity, which I considered very important for AWC's success. I will always be grateful to her for being open and honest with me in that moment.

There were times when I heard from women who, upon receiving one of my many promotional emails, would express their regret for not attending AWC's events. They often had a variety of reasons why they hadn't attended but liked that they got to read about each event and see pictures. I was always grateful and delighted to hear from them because they were supportive and served as ambassadors by talking positively about AWC and sending referrals our way. My response was always very personal and upbeat and hopeful that they would have the opportunity to join us at a future event. They appreciated our exchange. I could have been hurt and angry that they didn't attend an event, which is typical of many African group leaders, but I chose to trust that each woman was doing what was best for her. I wanted to assure her that whenever she found the time, I would be happy to have her presence and participation. The women appreciated not feeling pressured to be a part of AWC and, at the same time, being encouraged to keep in touch whenever possible.

Creating a group affirmation that everyone could recite at each meeting was another great way to keep things upbeat and positive. It also helped to remind people of what AWC is all about. The affirmation was a way to keep everyone at the event grounded in terms of our purpose for coming together. It also helped us hold ourselves and each other accountable to the purpose and values of AWC. Each time we recited the affirmation as a group, there was a recognition of what we could aspire to do together. The AWC affirmation was popular with the women, and I am proud to be the author of something that contributed greatly to creating a sense of positivity and togetherness.

An organization led by Africans serving Africans does not have to be divisive with a constant cloud of suspicion hovering over its leadership and participants. No one is perfect. Humans are complicated and often live with baggage from our upbringing and life experiences. However, self-awareness and being intentional about making a change can make a huge difference in what we can achieve.

Chapter 6

BEING OPEN TO THE POSSIBILITIES

B eing open to ideas, being spontaneous, and thinking on my feet are all things that don't come easily for me. I am the kind of person who is very comfortable with planning and organizing in advance. I am the one brainstorming multiple scenarios and finding solutions in case something out of the ordinary should occur. When I am planning an event, I usually have specific end results in mind, and if I don't get my desired results, I feel like I failed. In other words, I don't like leaving anything to chance.

I tend to be rather direct about things, and I'm not shy to ask for exactly what I want. Unfortunately, as you can imagine, not everyone is comfortable with my directness. Even worse, Africans are generally indirect in how they talk and act.

Fortunately for me, I've worked with some smart, wonderful, and selfless people who have taught me that being open doesn't have to be a scary thing. Whenever I think about being open to possibilities, I think of one particular situation.

I was a part of a small team of employees charged to plan our organization's staff holiday party. As is typical with nonprofits, we had a small budget and needed donations to get additional resources to have a successful event. One of our strategies was to send out request letters to businesses in our service area asking for in-kind donations. I suggested for our organizing team to make a list of all the things we wanted and then match the items to the business most likely to respond favorably to the request. For those who we couldn't match to donation items, I suggested that we ask for financial support to purchase whatever was needed. A kind and smart colleague, who had a lot more experience in planning such events than I did, explained that taking my approach would most likely limit options for the donors. She said that from her experience, donors usually came up with creative ways to assist when given the opportunity. That was a good lesson that putting people "in a box" can limit their ability to contribute, and they can surprise you when given a choice.

AWC was all about the possibilities. I wanted to create a safe, engaging, and welcoming space for networking and connecting. My hope was that the connections would lead to unimaginable possibilities and bring about all kinds of positive outcomes. I didn't want to get in the way of the women, and I certainly didn't want to put them in a box. I tried to accomplish this by experimenting with different formats to see what worked well.

I tried a range of themes, topics, and activities to engage, inspire, and connect people. I designed AWC so that women would choose how they participated, providing multiple ideas and options to stay engaged. I encouraged people to bring friends to have the experience together, I incorporated icebreaker activities to get everyone to participate, and I provided speakers, entertainment, outings, etc. I was constantly introducing something new and different. I got feedback and input, made changes to what wasn't working, and kept things that were working well. At times, it felt like a never-ending experiment, but it also kept things interesting.

Just like it took some time for me to learn how to be open to possibilities, I quickly found that many African women also found it challenging. I was asked repeatedly, "Where is all this networking leading to?" Eventually, it became clear that many were more comfortable with a plan and a simple and predictable endgame.

My goal was to provide a safe space for women to form AWC organically according to their needs, desires, expertise, and dreams. Not everyone understood what was being asked of them, and some were not comfortable with the concept of "building as you go." Most people were familiar with the nonprofit format—providing programs and services restricted by funding streams—or for profit format—providing products or services for at a price to make a profit. The fact that AWC was neither one nor the other was perplexing for some people.

Through feedback surveys and one-on-one conversations, I heard complaints about AWC not having a "real focus." I tried my hardest to make necessary adjustments according to comments and results from feedback information. Of course, we could not accommodate every single suggestion and didn't try to.

Being open to the possibilities certainly had both positives and negatives for AWC. After reflecting on all of the great work and connections that happened over those years, I found that AWC's goal was realized. AWC was new and unique, and its value was created by the women for themselves and the larger community. All of the trials and errors resulted in the realization that when we come together, we can discover greater personal and communal possibilities.

Chapter 7

BEING KIND, WELCOMING, AND FRIENDLY

From personal experience, many Africans have a hard time being kind, welcoming, and friendly to their fellow Africans. Because many Africans strongly believe in karma, they are generally kind and generous to the less fortunate and strangers. When someone is in dire need of onetime assistance, Africans are usually willing to step up and help. However, just being kind and friendly off the bat is not generally our strong feat.

There are several reasons why many Africans have difficulty being kind and generous. This includes, but is not limited to, cultural values and beliefs, upbringing, and a series of historical traumas due to things like poverty, colonization, oppression, etc. Growing up in Africa, I quickly became aware that those who were thriving and doing well were primarily those who had the most power, resources, and access to opportunities necessary to be successful such as quality education, healthcare, employment, and the like. On the other hand, those who didn't fare so well were people who were powerless with little or no resources and access. The latter group usually had little, if any, control over the trajectory of their lives unless something extraordinary happened. I'm not judging but merely stating the facts as I lived and experienced it.

I believe that when we know, we must change and do better. It takes a lot of practice to relearn how to think and what actions we should take. When we fail to change, the typical African values and beliefs that are negative in nature can ultimately derail our efforts to build healthy and beneficial relationships with others.

It was paramount to keep this background in mind when I led AWC. There were times when I approached women — with a positive attitude and my most charming smile — and they responded with a snobbish attitude that said, "Who are you anyway, and why are you talking to me?" In those moments, I reminded myself not to take it personally. It was just the way people typically reacted to their fellow Africans who are unfamiliar to them. Developing hard feelings because of people's negative attitudes were going to get me nowhere close to the goals set for AWC.

I understood that in order to run an organization like AWC successfully, I needed the buy in of the people. It was critical to be approachable and treat people with kindness and respect no matter the response, especially from people who needed a compelling reason to sign on to the idea of AWC. Most of the time, the less than friendly response from women was demonstrated only during initial meetings. Once they noticed that they could not scare me away so easily, they softened up and became more open to hearing me out.

I learned to do some of the following things:

- **Be curious about people, including their hopes and dreams:** I found out personal information about people and what motivated them. I did this by listening intently when people talked and by talking less. It also helped when I shared something about myself too—preferably matching what they shared.

- **Learn about their most important needs and provide any support possible:** I kept what people told me at the back of my mind and tried to help in any way I could, whether immediately or in the future. Sometimes just knowing their interests provided opportunities to send relevant referrals or just to share in their interests.

- **Show understanding and compassion:** Whether or not they were on board with AWC, it was important for me to remember that people are individuals first. Also, we all have complex lives that demand meeting on a human level no matter what.

- **Respect personal decisions:** I tried to do this without providing unsolicited advice and information. Whenever we respect a person's decision, it leads to mutual respect, and the gesture is not easily forgotten.

- **Understand that it may not be the best time for the person:** I noticed that when I gave people the space and time they needed to decide, they greatly appreciated it. Once they were ready to engage, I made sure to respond in a positive way. This goes hand in hand with respecting their decisions. If their circumstances change or they rethink your offer, they'll seek you out. Sometimes they will even gladly share your story with others and refer to you others who are interested.

- **Be genuinely interested in people's health, happiness, and dreams:** I did my best to be supportive of people. Empathize, sympathize, and celebrate with people as appropriate. You can do this well if you consciously live in the present and are attentive instead of thinking about your next move.

Being kind and friendly sounds simple and logical, but it's not always easy, especially when it's not something that you are accustomed to doing. At any given moment, my mind is constantly processing the many ideas that run through it. I often have to consciously work at staying in the present when I'm engaging with people. When I get distracted, I make it a point to apologize if needed, ask questions, or get clarification. Everyone appreciates kindness and friendliness.

Chapter 8

BEING INCLUSIVE

Africa is the world's second largest and second most populous continent. Today, Africa contains fifty-four sovereign countries and a hosts a large diversity of ethnicities, cultures, and languages. Africans profess a wide variety of religious beliefs, and statistics on religious affiliation are difficult to come by since it is often a sensitive topic for governments with mixed religious populations. According to Encyclopedia Britannica, 45 percent of the population consists of Christians, 40 percent are Muslims, and 10 percent follow traditional religions. A small number of Africans are Hindu, Buddhist, Confucianist, Baha'i, or Jewish. There is also a minority of Africans who are irreligious.

For these reasons and more, attempting to work with a community of African immigrants remains a challenging undertaking. There were no manuals on best practices to reference. It was all done on the basis of "feel it out and keep what sticks, works, or makes the most sense." My goal was to go with what was most common to most women and rely on the social norms in African immigrant communities in the United States in general and Minnesota specifically.

One of the things that I decided early on was that the focus would be on women's lives in the United States, not on the African continent. Some people were not happy about this focus. Many were used to gathering as people from a particular country or ethnic group and working on projects to assist people on the continent. Those were all wonderful endeavors, and some were very impactful.However, they were specific to only a particular group of people.

Imagine AWC looking to do one project on the continent. Where and how would the project be implemented, and who would it benefit? Would it be voted on by the participants or the leadership of AWC? Obviously, people would favor their own countries and what they perceive as the pressing issues, which would be greatly influenced by family and friends back home. Since the continent is experiencing many problems, how would it be decided which country or region would get priority? These questions demonstrate precisely why focusing on the African continent would have most likely brought about disharmony among AWC's participants.

Getting to know the ladies, I often learned about the great work and projects that they were doing individually and collectively on the ground in Africa. I was always happy to have them share their stories with the group. It was important to help everyone understanding that the sharing was only for information and promotion, but no one was obligated to contribute or support the endeavor. As the leader of a diverse group of people who were challenged in many ways, it was my responsibility to ensure people didn't lose sight of the main purpose of AWC—to expand their network, learn, and build relationships.

AWC had participants who were independent consultants and small business owners. This group of entrepreneurs was always looking to grow their customer base, and AWC had potential customers. Considering that they were looking to sell products and services to the AWC audience, I constantly had to explain the importance of not placing any pressure or guilt on people who simply wanted to mingle because it could drive them away. There were also people who wanted to provide information about nonprofit programs and services. Inviting them to join the group and asking them not to market at the event was a constant balancing act. I didn't want to open the doors to a parade of promoters and sales people who could likely annoy participants and eventually drive them away.

I often encouraged people to focus their time at AWC on building relationships primarily. My experience with building relationships is that once people get to know you on a personal basis, they get to know you as a friend and would be a more willing prospect. Unfortunately, most people came to AWC events hoping for a quick fix and did not want to take the time needed to build long-term relationships with potential customers or clients.

To ease things a little, the AWC Market Day Event was created, where entrepreneurs could pay to be vendors and have exhibit booths at the biggest event of the year—AWC's Annual Holiday Dinner. In addition, I encouraged the women to make presentations as experts and make a soft ask at the end by sharing contact information or setting up appointment dates for after the AWC event. This strategy did not make everyone happy, but it was a good compromise. It helped fill the need for speakers and subject matter experts.

One thing I found that was very common with most communities was that religious faith and spirituality were important to most women. Very often, people wanted to start the meeting off with a word of prayer, and knowing that we sometimes had women outside of the Christian faith in our midst, I found a prayer that I thought was appropriate for our purpose, made some adjustments, and came up with an inclusive "prayer" for everyone.

Although AWC participants lived in the United States, they were just as diverse as people are on the continent of Africa; they come from different countries, ethnicities, and cultures and speak various languages and have diverse values. There were no reference guides on how to build a group of diverse African women. Through experimentation, observation, and gut feeling, I was able to generate interests by building on what was most common as well as relying on the social norms in African immigrant communities in the United States in general and Minnesota in particular.

Chapter 9

Keeping Time—Not African Time

"African time" is a big issue in African immigrant communities abroad. This refers to Africans having a more relaxed attitude regarding punctuality, whereas in Western cultures such as the United States, time is managed stringently with little or no flexibility. It doesn't matter how long Africans live abroad, when it comes to community events organized by Africans for Africans, they keep "African time." Tardiness can range anywhere from a half hour to one or two hours. For the most part, it is expected and acceptable by many in the community to the point where event hosts often plan for a later program start due to the expectation that about half of the guests would arrive late. However, it can be very frustrating for non-African guests in attendance. I have had experiences where extra time is added on before the actual start time in hopes that those running a few minutes late will actually arrive on time. For example, a 5:45 pm start time is really 6:00 pm, and at times, the host would go to lengths to have different invitations printed to target different audiences. In this case, the African community would be given the invitation with the 5:45 pm start time, and the mainstream community would be given the invitation with the 6:00 pm start time.

Personally, I consider anything more than a half hour rude and unacceptable. It is a waste of people's time and disrespectful to the host and other guests who arrive on time. Some regard "African time" as part of the African culture and therefore okay. The fact is that "African time" results in unsuccessful events that go on for way too long to allow for people to trickle in. These run-through-style events are not enjoyable because there are never enough people at one time for socializing in a meaningful way.

When it comes to event planning, people who don't keep time are costly and problematic. For one thing, venues are often priced by the hour, and the more time needed for an event, the costlier it will be. I have attended catered events where food was scheduled to be served at a certain time of the day relative to RSVPs or as reported by the host. Due to African's relaxed attitude towards time, the food went to waste because the number of people present was much less than the reservation number. Funds are not reimbursed when this happens.

RSVP'ing for an event is another thing that is not generally considered "African" in immigrant communities. People are often late responding by the deadline or may think that receiving an invitation is in itself enough to guarantee them a place at the event. The argument is that RSVP'ing is about preferential treatment of certain groups and is also used to bring about shame around something that should be celebratory, lighthearted, and fun.

With AWC, I decided that the run-through-style event was not a good format. Women generally have busy lives and no time to sit around waiting for things to happen. Responsibilities often included work, school, taking care of children, spouses, and extended family members on the continent and abroad, second jobs, interests and hobbies, running on the side businesses, religious community participation, community leadership, civic engagement, and nonprofit work.

I remember one AWC participant who confided that she was solely responsible for putting her sister through college in Africa. This woman was in her twenties and in graduate school, working a full-time job and a second job taking care of a senior citizen on evenings and weekends. Without her help, her sister would not have been able to achieve a college education. She was also helping to support other family members. This AWC participant's story was similar to many others. They were the lifeline of their families.

My family home was AWC's first meeting space. It was a convenient and affordable start, but I remember thinking that the gatherings were more social than I had planned. Somehow the home setting made people feel really comfortable, and it felt like a group of friends paying me a visit instead of the purposeful networking event it was intended to be. One year later, I decided to move AWC out of my home and quickly found that renting a meeting space was costly. Meeting spaces had to be reserved or rented. There was no meeting space that offered unlimited meeting hours for free or even at an affordable rate. When we used restaurants or free spaces, we had to purchase food and drinks and make sure not to overstay our welcome, prevent the establishment from generating income, or negatively impact customer service.

I knew there was a lot to compete with when it came to the women's time. I wanted to respect their time and be trusted to deliver a great experience in the two to four hours that they had so graciously entrusted me. I always planned an agenda for the time we met and stuck to it religiously. I made sure to get them out the door on time having done everything I had promised.

If we were meeting at a restaurant or at a public setting, I visited the space prior to the event day. I did a walkthrough of the space, made any necessary special seating arrangements, including requesting additional tables and chairs or specific furniture set up, reviewed the food order, etc. I also did a walkthrough of available parking and traffic in the area, which were most likely included in event communications to participants. I also did whatever shopping was needed in order for the event to run smoothly on the day and ensure it started and ended on time while meeting expectations and following through with our promises.

The event plan usually included me and a volunteer, if available, and we would get to the venue thirty minutes to one hour before start time. I made sure the agreed upon arrangements had been carried out as planned. There were times when the desired set up looked different than during the walk through, so changes had to be made. I also made sure to be present and ready to greet guests as they arrived. Things like sign-in forms, pens, and name tags also had to be ready before the women started arriving.

It was important to have copies of the agenda of the day so the women could follow and know what to expect. The agenda generally included twenty minutes to a half hour for mingling and networking followed by welcome and logistics. Next, we recited the "thankful prayer" (written copies were available on tables or in the program), and then time was allowed for introductions or an icebreaker activity. The main speaker or featured topic took anywhere from thirty to forty minutes, including Q&A and announcing the next meeting date. I tried to wrap up five to ten minutes early to allow time for completing the satisfaction survey, saying goodbyes, or leaving early for those who had to quickly make it to another engagement.

The women liked that I was prepared and organized. They trusted my word and were comfortable following my lead even when I led them to unfamiliar territory.The true reward for me was having more people come on time because they knew we were going to start and end on time.

Africans generally have a hard time ending events, especially when they have had a great time. That's usually when we want to talk about all that just happened and then some, but it was not always possible to stick around and talk. In fact, there were times when I had to shoo people out of some establishments because others had to come in after us, which some found to be un-African. I was fine with taking the talking outside to the parking lot for as long as they wanted because it was on their personal time. That way I couldn't be blamed for keeping them later than expected.

Although I took pride in keeping time, unfortunately, some participants considered it to be one of the things that proved AWC was elitist and not "African" enough. That is understandable when looking at it from a cultural perspective, where attitudes around time and punctuality are more relaxed. There are definitely benefits to being more flexible with time especially when it comes to building relationships. It takes time to get to know someone and build trust. Thankfully, AWC events were ongoing and I was intentional about sharing a schedule of event dates in advance so attendees knew that there were many more opportunities to meetup again.

Chapter 10

PROVIDING OPPORTUNITIES
FOR PERSONAL GROWTH

I was intentional about providing opportunities for women to develop, improve, and grow through AWC. If women were going to invest a couple of hours out of their busy schedules to attend AWC events, I wanted to ensure they had a good time but also a valuable experience.

Bringing in topic experts to encourage the women to explore new thingsor improve their skills wasaway AWC added value to their lives for the time they invested. We did numerous things, including information on financial planning, professional coaching, mentorship, goal setting, networking, creating a personal elevator speech, assessing nonprofit board participation, small business banking, and healthy relationships.

AWC organized various group trips to art performances around the city. One of the many memorable trips was to the

Minneapolis Institute of Arts (MIA) to tour the African galleries. Even though many of the artworks on display were pretty familiar to the women, it was interesting for them to see them displayed in a museum and to read the historical write-ups accompanying the pieces. It was also exciting to have the experience as a group and to get the chance to see parts of the history of Africa from a new and different perspective. It was great to observe and hear other museum visitors' perspectives on the items as well. The group tour guide was MIA's volunteer and an AWC participant as well. She was able to expertly blend her own knowledge, experience, and interests with the information provided by the MIA and her rapport with the women, which made for a fantastic experience for the group! She was given a one of a kind opportunity through AWC to share her knowledge, passion, and expertise of the arts, model volunteering for AWC participants, and enjoy her time with a unique group of visitors she hadn't assisted before.

Other experiences included theatre performancesand intentionally supporting minority-owned small businesses by hosting AWC events at their establishments. This was a great way to model community support while, at the same time, providing new or enriching experiences for the participants. The intentional support of local and immigrant-owned businesses was also so that the women would become aware of those businesses and hopefully continue to support them outside of AWC as well as recommend them to others.

Another group experience included volunteering with a local battered women's shelter. AWC's group spent time reading to the kids, prepared an African inspired dinner, and chatted with the residents. The opportunity was made possible by an AWC participant who was also a staff licensed psychologist at the shelter.

One of AWC participants had a dream to start an orphanage in Rwanda, her country of origin. AWC was able to support her dream and passion for several years by organizing a group of volunteers to assist with a yearly fundraiser that supported the orphanage work in Rwanda. It was amazing to watch her dream start as a plan in the form of a drawing, grow to a plot of land, and build up from bricks to buildings to a village of children, adults, supporters, and a host of donors. What a wonderful thing to experience as a group and be inspired by her success! Some AWC participants continue to be a part of this project today.

AWC provided information and trainings that some of the women would not have had access to otherwise. The board service participation training mentioned earlier included important points to consider and do before joining a board. I remember that several women in attendance at the training said that the information was timely and helpful. They learned a lot that they hadn't thought about before and were going to implement some of what they had learned immediately.

Participants received presentations, written information, and talks on networking skills, and each AWC event provided an opportunity to practice those skills. Training was also provided on how to create an elevator speech for personal and work-related purposes, and participants used a worksheet to craft their elevator speech and worked in pairs to practice and get comfortable using that skill before leaving the session.

Opportunities to grow varied from formal training to practical participatory formats. At AWC events, each woman was encouraged to introduce herself and respond to icebreaker questions, engage in activities, share information relevant to the group or topic, mingle, get to know someone new, and build deeper relationships.

There were situations where some of the women got a chance to refer each other for community projects and initiatives outside of AWC. They got to know the women not only as friends but also as professionals and did not hesitate to make appropriate verbal and written referrals. A few women served on boards and committees together beyond AWC, and things like job openings were frequently shared among AWC participants.

The participants often shared with me their appreciation for finding and building a network of professional women like themselves that they could refer and share information and opportunities with when needed. Many of these women had access to influential individuals and unique opportunities. Some did not have other professionals who were African immigrant women in their circle to turn to when needed. Invitations and opportunities to professional events as well as various complimentary tickets and trips from employers were exchanged many times between participants who were glad that they had finally found people who could benefit from what they had to offer.

AWC provided a safe space to ask questions and have meaningful discussions about various topics around community and personal issues. Not much of our conversations could be replicated or duplicated in any other settings. AWC goals and objectives were uniquely designed to meet the needs of its target audience and expand their horizons. The experience was uniquely AWC's.

The growth could be seen and felt in the women who frequently attended AWC events and engaged intentionally. They became more comfortable with the organizational format and sought out deeper engagement through their interactions, questions, suggestions, increased levels of participation, and more importantly, their activities beyond AWC events.

Chapter 11

NOT TAKING THINGS PERSONALLY

When it comes to selling an idea, rejection is most often directed towards the idea itself and not the salesperson. Unfortunately, I can't say that is true for selling an idea to African people in general, especially when the salesperson is a fellow African. With this group, rejection often has to do with the salesperson.

This kind of rejection has to do with any number of things. It could be because the salesperson is unfamiliar; they are from a different country-ethnic group, place of worship, economic status, etc., or they have an inadequate education level, unacceptable appearance, and so on.

Getting buy in from African women to join AWC was often more difficult than from those who were not Africans. My job would have been a lot easier had I changed my target audience, but that was never the plan or even a consideration. My sole desire was to design and build an organization by and for African women to connect.

I had to find a way to look past rejection and keep working towards my goal. I made a conscious decision to not take rejections personally even when they seemed blatantly personal. There were many times when I felt like I was being interviewed for a position. In a way, it was a leadership position, and it was important to some that I met their expectation, whether or not I considered it fair. I was determined not to let rejection and intense interrogation discourage my progress by practicing the following steps:

1. Dig deeper by asking the question "Why?"
2. Regard "no" as "not right now"
3. Find other paths back to the beginning (hit the restart button)
4. Let it go if things don't change
5. Shake it off and move on (live and learn)
6. Don't hold a grudge

Dig deeper by asking the question "Why?"

When people said "no," I politely and courteously helped them dig deeper to get to the reason why. If possible, I would then figure out how I could help them get to "maybe" or "yes." For example, after giving my best pitch of AWC, the person replied, "That sounds like a great idea but no thanks." In that response, I saw that as a high potential for persuasion. I might respond with, "What part of the idea do you find great?" Or say, "Obviously, you think it is a great idea, so I don't understand why you decided not to participate. Please tell me why." If the person was open to providing an explanation, I was usually able to keep the conversation going. If I could not convince them to try AWC, I would at least get them closer to a "maybe."

Responding in that way also helped me to improve my pitch and to adjust my marketing approach. When someone shared a point that really helped me see a different perspective, I made sure to tell them that. I've never met anyone who doesn't enjoy hearing that they helped someone rethink or improve something. It is flattering and a surefire way to boost people's ego and make them feel valuable. One thing I learned quickly about African women is that they love to tell it like it is, which turned out to be a wonderful thing for me and AWC. I received many valuable ideas this way.

Regard "no" as "not right now"

People can always change their minds. They usually need time to think, make observations, get different perspectives, and reconsider if needed. One way to help with this is to offer additional information, ask if you could contact them at a future time, or extend an open invitation to join you in the future. Exchanging contact information allows a reasonable distance while continuing to make contact through email, phone, regular mail, etc. Providing much needed space and time while sharing information could present a more opportune time in the future.

Find other paths back to the beginning

Maybe the timing was all wrong. Whether from your end or theirs, there is a good chance that things would have a different result if the circumstances were different. Acknowledge if necessary and look for a better opportunity to revisit. Basically, you would have to reset the process, which could include finding a more appropriate messenger who might be more familiar or have a better connection to the person than you.

Let it go if things don't change

All you can do is your best. If things don't move along after attempting to find out why they won't get on board, providing additional information, giving them time to think things over, and trying to restart the process, let it go. Close the door but don't seal the lock. Take a breath, walk away, and focus on someone or something else.

Shake it off and move on

Don't allow rejection to get you down for a long period of time because it can lead to lost opportunities. Someone once told me that sales is a numbers game. The more people you can reach, the better your chances of landing a few. So if you get a buy in from one out of every five women, and you reach ten, you'll land two. And if you reach thirty, you will have a chance of landing six. Therefore, it would work to your advantage not to spend a lot of downtime being discouraged over one rejection. Also, remember that the ones you convince probably have a few friends that they could reach out to on your behalf. Be positive, and don't just imagine the possibilities but get on with it!

Don't hold a grudge

The worst thing you can do is hold a grudge against someone who turned down your offer. Remember that the decision usually has to do with the person's choice, which has nothing to do with what you want. Respect what people want for themselves. Be professional. Take the high road because you just never know—things could turn around, circumstances could change, minds could change—and you could find yourself with another opportunity to retry. Don't burn bridges or lock doors. It could come back to hunt you!

Nothing worth having comes easy. Rejection is difficult no matter the motivation. When you're trying to get people to accept what you're offering them, you have to be ready for both a positive and negative response. African women proved to be a difficult group to convince in general. However, with the right attitude and strategies, it is possible to succeed.

Chapter 12

BEING CREATIVE AND INNOVATIVE

Thankfully, I am naturally a creative and innovative person. Those attributes came in handy in founding and leading AWC. I came upon the idea of AWC thinking that I could make it happen with little or no significant financial costs without serious consideration of the nonfinancial costs (opportunity costs) like time and energy and foregoing things, which if quantified, would be substantial and burdensome. My computer skills and the fact that I'm a quick study helped me tremendously. In addition, my knowledge, organizational skills, and experiences in the corporate world made me efficient in implementing event planning activities, marketing promotions, and communication strategies.

Since AWC was a job where I did not have to report to a supervisor or worry about performance reviews, I felt no pressure or fear of failure. I was passionate about the idea of

AWC and was willing to work hard and figure it out. I was excited about the freedom to be as creative and innovative as I desired. Back then, I had not had any paid work that provided opportunities for me to use my creative skills to the level AWC did.

For many of the decisions I made, I had to follow my gut. Since there were no manuals or someone to bounce ideas off of, I had to learn how to rely on what felt right. Over the years, I learned to trust my gut feeling, and I discovered that a majority of the time, my gut feeling is spot on. Now I know that my intuition is one of my best assets.

I was often asked who created my flyers, brochures, invitations, etc. I did it all myself because 1) I couldn't afford to pay for design and creative services, 2) I didn't have a lot of time to devote to creative planning because it had to happen in the midst of work, family life, and whatever else had to be done, and 3) it was all in my head, and I didn't think anyone could have come up with similar ideas.

My writing skills came in handy and I did a lot of it! Outside of events and meetings, most of my communication with the women was in written format. Creating messages that resonated with the audience was important and knowing when to reuse, rewrite or create a new message to match each situation was important. To do this, I had to pay attention to what was happening at events, what the women were saying when we got together, what they shared through the surveys, how they interacted with each other, etc. I remember that I wrote a piece titled "10 Reasons Why People Come to AWC

Events" that received a lot of positive feedback. The list included to get a life, for a girls date night, as prelude to a night out on the town, to put a face on their business, to support community, to meet experienced professionals, to meet others like themselves, to practice their networking skills, to get resources and information unique to them, and to brush up on their people skills. These were all things that I observed and heard from AWC participants and that is why it got the feedback it did. I could not have done this effectively without having the skill and knowledge to be creative. Having lots of opportunities to practice didn't hurt either.

Images used to promote AWC were also intentional. It was important to ensure the audience could see and feel a reflection of themselves in the images. I spent a considerable amount of time looking for images and clipart online that reflected my audience's features and values—which were not many to choose from. They had to be free because I did not have the money to purchase nicer stock photos from online picture libraries. Luckily, I found one clipart of two women with African features, which I used repeatedly on event flyers during the first year AWC was established. Once I developed the first logo, which was drawn by hand and then cut out on dark paper to create a silhouette effect to finish the look, I started using the logo instead of the clipart. Pictures taken at AWC events were used in blog posts and newsletters and as a result they got a higher than average number of clicks. Sharing events pictures also helped increase the number of new participants.

Part of using my creativity was looking for the most affordable ways to get messages out in a way that led to great results and accomplished set goals. Social media presented a variety of exciting new ways to do that at little or no cost. For example, we used Evite™, a free online event management program. Having an account meant that AWC's contact information was stored. I could segment participants and send targeted communicate to participants as needed. Automated functions made it easy to add and delete people, keep tract of RSVPs, have a two-way conversation, and send reminders and updates in a timely manner.

Free blog platforms allowed me to share stories about AWC and keep a repository of stories and pictures that participants and the general public could access conveniently. Facebook, Twitter, and LinkedIn allowed me to continue to support and share stories about African women with those interested, as well as provide an opportunity for women to connect through social media. Survey Monkey allowed AWC to get feedback and share it in an effective way.

We had to pay for services like an email marketing site that allowed us to send electronic emails to dozens of people all at once. The skills needed to build and maintain a website was way beyond my abilities and time. The investment to maintain a website and ensure it was up and running smoothly proved to be challenging and outside of my budget.

AWC's Meetup site was fee based. It allowed AWC to expand its reach online, which resulted in increased interests and a few new attendees.

Creativity and innovation were invaluable in getting AWC communications to the women in ways that were relatable, affordable, engaging, and effective. It took a lot of ingenuity, time, and energy, but it helped realize AWC's goal of staying connected in multiple ways while building and strengthening relationships.

Chapter 13

BEING BRAVE AND BOLD

I enjoy the pageantry of political campaigns. The amount of hard work, high energy, toughness, and tenacity exhibited during a political campaign is amazing. However, I would in no way, shape, or form want to take the place of any of the candidates because of the level of scrutiny and attacks that comes with the territory. With all that, I admire the men and women who bravely get into the race knowing that it will require a fight for their ideas, beliefs, reputation, records, values, history, and more. They have to put themselves out there and demand the opportunity to make a compelling case. They have to convince the voters that they are indeed the right candidate with the best ideas and the best person to fight for their values and desires. And if they successfully make the case, they garner the votes needed to win the race.

Forming and leading AWC came nowhere close to running a political campaign, but I discovered that I had to think like a

Rita Jackson Apaloo

campaigner to convince people to buy in to the idea of working together for the good of the individual as well as the community. People needed to know my story, including my background and what qualified me to do the work. They had a lot of questions about how things were going to work and who was going to be responsible for what. Just like it takes bravery and boldness to thrive in a campaign situation, I had to apply similar strategies, though on a much smaller scale of intensity.

Before setting out to talk to people about AWC, I had to get my story together. I knew that the AWC concept of bringing African women of all backgrounds and nationalities together was not being done because of the challenges of differences in culture, values, desires, community norms, and more. I needed to develop key messages that appealed to different ideas and audiences. I also developed elevator speeches to use in situations where I had very little time to pitch AWC to a potential participant or ally. Once I felt satisfied with the messages and pitches, I strategized my communicated about AWC and made the necessary adjustments on an ongoing basis.

Believe it or not, I am an introvert. Yes, that's right. I am. No, I'm not the shy, anxious, or antisocial kind. I am the kind of introvert that is sociable, thinking, and reserved. That means I'm never the hugely popular person or the one who's the life of the party. I also did not have a long list of friends I could call on to join AWC, which was somewhat worrisome in the beginning.

But one thing I had going for me, I believe, was my temperament, my respectful interactions with people, and my willingness to get involved and contribute in several community initiatives and efforts. People who knew me and had worked with me knew that I was a person they could rely on to get things done. They felt that I was trustworthy, delivered on my promises, and had good intentions to do the right thing.

I had worked with and befriended some women from various African countries and communities that I could reach out to. I also frequented events that I could plan to setup a recruiting table at where there was a mix of Africans from different communities. Once I thought about potential recruits and made a list of people who I could ask to help out, I felt I had what I needed to start AWC.

The plan was to get the word out about AWC primarily to women who were regarded as influencers and opinion leaders in their communities. I couldn't find these individuals on my own, so I asked for help from family and friends. I provided my volunteers with information and key messages of AWC while making sure they had access to resources like business cards, flyers, and online sites.

To capture people's interests in terms of what we could address together, I talked about social issues experienced by many African women. One idea was that the public generally had a negative view of African women, and we could change that by building a community and working to change the narrative. Another idea was that African women often held stereotypes about one another that have prevented us from working together and building successful coalitions. AWC's aim was to provide opportunities to help women get to know one another better and build meaningful relationships.

It was important to be positive, empathetic, patient, understanding, and welcoming at all stages in communicating about AWC, no matter what. After years of dreaming about the idea of AWC, it was important to find the courage to make it happen. It wasn't a concept that was around or familiar to people, so the difficulty was articulating my ideas in a way that got people interested and excited about what I had to offer. I had to toughen up against the naysayers and rumor mongers and nonbelievers and not take things personally.

I had to learn to pay close attention to how things were unfolding with AWC so that I could retell the successes but also find solutions for the problems and concerns people had. I never turned on the ones who spoke up or shared their questions, concerns, or feelings because in many ways, they were my consultants and focus group that helped me improve on my ideas and plan.

I couldn't change, fix, or refute things that people were concerned with unless I knew what they were, which was by people being comfortable enough to tell me or share through the various feedback channels.

Another important aspect of a campaign-like structure is giving credit where and when it is due. No man is an island, and there was no way I could have single-handedly recruited for and managed AWC. I always took the time to thank people and acknowledge them privately and publicly. This included attendees because they were integral to AWC's success just as the volunteers and supporters were. Every person's role was important to AWC's success.

When things weren't going as planned, strategic sessions were sometimes held with others I trusted and many times just by me, myself, and I. Were things going as planned? Was it time to try something new? There were times when I decided to keep going, and there were times when I wasn't sure if I should stay in the "race." However, just like campaigns usually do, when it got to the point where it was clear that the costs outweighed the benefits of the mission, I had to be honest with myself about my motivations to keep pushing forward.

In the end, when I determined that I needed a lot more than I had available financially and emotionally and that the "race" couldn't be won without more sacrifice than I was willing to make, I turned in the towel and called it a day well spent with no regrets.

Chapter 14

MAKING IT RELEVANT

We live in an age where personalization, segmentation, and customization are expected. Gone are the days of one-size-fits all. Today, people expect things that fit what they want for themselves and provide choices and advantages unique to them without undue burden.

As an African, I'm used to people putting me in the "African" box, which can be annoying and frustrating. I have lost count of the times when people say to me, "You don't look or sound African." Sometimes they say, "I would have never guessed that you are African." How do you respond to such microaggressive behavior, especially when they seem so sincere and oblivious of the impact of their words? I used to not respond at all, but nowadays, I turn such situations into teachable moments.

Rita Jackson Apaloo

Africans are some of the most diverse people in the world. First of all, as we try to remind people time and time again, Africa is not a country. It is continent with fifty-four different countries. Secondly, there are a lot of differences in terms of culture, tradition, beliefs, values, food, dress, language, etc. There are additional differences among people regionally within a country and even within ethnic groups. I was never referred to as an African until I lived in the United States, so I have had to learn how to respond to that label. The African label could mean a lot of different things, depending on who's saying it and in what context it is being said.

Let's be real. Stereotyping happens among Africans too, and very rampantly, I may add. I remember when a friend and AWC participant confided that she often hesitates to tell people that she is Nigerian because of the many stereotypes people have about Nigerian people. I was honored that she trusted me enough to share her personal concern with me. That has stayed with me and motivated me even more to not let assumptions or stereotypes affect how I treat others, specifically the women I was trying to engage.

This is not to say we should ignore universal values and cultures of a particular group of people because they can be relevant. However, we need to be careful not to use it as a blanket approach that is applied to individuals or a group of people, especially if used to discriminate. It is important to find out what's unique about a person and what's important to them.

AWC participants were at different stages of their personal journeys, so things that were relevant for some women were not necessarily the same for others. Some were business owners looking for resources and connections with other entrepreneurs. Some were executives in their organizations or leading nonprofit organizations. Others were managers and supervisors on their jobs, while others were just starting their careers or looking to grow. All of the women had different needs but supported one another, learned from each other, and appreciated AWC's efforts in managing the diverse needs and talents.

Ensuring that AWC continued to be relevant to the women included providing opportunities for feedback on events and activities. I also consistently encouraged them to provide suggestions regarding what AWC could try or do differently. It is true that you can't please all people all the time. However, listening, acknowledging, and responding to people can help gain support and develop trust. Discouraging feedback does the opposite and is most likely to result in disengagement.

Audience segmentation can be time consuming, and one will have to be knowledgeable and skilled to get good results. My public relations background came in handy in creating audience profiles, crafting messages, making decisions about communication channels, etc. My approach was to use a broad appeal strategy to get women in the door, but after that, I had to figure out what their perception of the organization was and what their aspirations were for joining the group. That feedback allowed me to craft my message to them appropriately and successfully.

Customization was key in building relationships and making people feel special and not just lumped with everyone else. It took more time and creativity, but the results were amazing and rewarding. Something as simple as responding to an email or returning a call can go a long ways in helping people feel heard and listened to. For example, when someone responded to a thank you message I sent after an event, I made sure to respond right away and specifically responded to things they alluded to in their email. I also sent messages to those who did not attend, letting them know that they were missed. The messaged included links to a summary and pictures from the event they missed.

People would often respond and let me know why they didn't make it. Most of the time it had to do with nothing more than the run-of-the-mill busyness of life, to which I politely responded with understanding and expressed my hope that they would have an opportunity to join us soon. This practice went a long way in building and maintaining relationships with women interested in AWC.

It's easier to personalize communication when you take the time to know your audience. Knowing specific information like their interests, occupation, family status, country of origin, etc., are critical. When you can remember these things and weave them into conversations and written communication, you will begin to build meaningful and lasting relationships.

Chapter 15

BEING ENGAGING AND INTERACTIVE

People expect more because of the abundance of information and opportunities all around us. They are getting all kinds of information and requests coming at them constantly, many of which they ignore unless they feel connected or interested for some compelling reason. Research shows that people respond to something that challenges them, like an offer, or something that speaks to them.

AWC intrigued African women because of its promises to assist them in connecting with people like themselves to expand their network for friendship, business, and community. African women are tremendously curious about each other. They usually want to know how they are different and how they are similar with the other person.

I know I've said this over and over again, but I can't stress enough the importance of feedback! It was important to hear back from people and be intentional about getting their input, especially because I was treading new waters.

Knowing that my target audience was a group of busy women with hectic lives at home, work, and in the community, I wanted to find a way to engage them despite their busy circumstances. Technology was the answer. It allowed me to engage in a way that was convenient to them. In addition, it was becoming the way more and more people were staying connected, so I began to use it quite aggressively.

In 2004, when AWC was founded, not many women in African immigrant communities had access to the internet or were comfortable using it. In fact, many of the first waves of AWC participants had access through their jobs, which meant they worked in professional settings or were students with access to the internet. I believe this is why there was some criticism about AWC catering mostly to a certain type of African women and not really open to all. The word "elitist" was used to describe AWC more than once because of my preference for written communication and my use of the internetas the predominate channel of communication.

I too worked in an office setting at the time and was in awe of the power of the internet and the possibilities social media presented. I was excited to have such tools at my fingertips. My hope was that the women with access to the internet would forward AWC emails, keep others in their network updated through word-of-mouth, and encourage their friends to join. It worked for the most part. Once someone attended a meeting, their contact information was collected, and they received ongoing communication from AWC. Participant records included a note about their preferred way to be contacted, which was also a question on the signup sheet. This was helpful and people appreciated that their wishes were respected.

A surefire way to increase engagement is to get people involved with planning and organizing an event. That is if you can convince them to do it. I found that convincing the women to commit to helping out on an ongoing basis was almost impossible because of their already busy lives. However, asking them to commit to a one-time project was not only enticing but also much easier for people to say yes. There was a start and end date that they could manage.

AWC's holiday event was the biggest and usually the most attended event each year. It was held in early December, a festive time of year, plus people are generally in the best of moods during the holiday season. A bigger event requires extra help in order for things to go smoothly so I would ask a couple of women to assist for the day. They were usually happy and willing to help make the day a success, which included doing their part to prepare for the day, getting there on time, inviting their friends to attend, and having a great time as well. The best part was watching the women do their thing and taking over and owning what and how they contributed to the event.

AWC's Leadership Summit was a special event that was held only once but it was also very different from the usual monthly events. It included a panel discussion and facilitated table conversations, which meant more hands were needed on deck to make it a success. Commitment for this event required more time because we had several meetings and people were assigned to complete tasks that were critical to the success of event planning and facilitation. I ensured that the women were recognized for their work by including their names and bios on the event written materials and encouraging them to have speaking and reporting roles during and after event. Getting involved in this way certainly increased their interests and engagement in the mission and vision of AWC more than before.

Intentionally asking women to serve as topicexperts and keynote speakers had the same effect as being a part of planning, organizing and leading events. Attendees always had a role to play as audience members, whether it was introducing themselves to others in the room, participating in an activity, or contributing to the discussion. AWC events were designed to promote engagement and interaction.

The different social media platforms allowed AWC to have constant contact with its audience. Using the social media tools was a great way to keep the women interested and provide plenty of opportunities to engage in a two-way communication.

However, face-to-face interactions remained an integral part of AWC's strategy, and it was also more impactful and more enjoyable than any of the many platforms used. Face-to-face events also provided opportunities for development through presentations, trainings, and other educational activities.

Social networking enhanced face-to-face meetings in that people were more familiar with each other. It helped people become more comfortable and ready to engage, including me, the host, who had had the most interactions with the women. Using technology also made it possible for me to have additional interactions with the women outside of events, which allowed me to be accessible to them whenever they needed.

Utilizing multiple channels of communication and engagement strategies provided numerous ways to reach women, promote the program and keep the lines of communication open in between face-to face events. Getting feedback and keeping connected on an ongoing basis were also benefits of using several communication channels. In addition, finding opportunities to deepened participants' involvement exponentially increased their engagement and sense of ownership of AWC's mission and goals.

Chapter 16

PROVIDING FOOD THAT MATTERS

When it comes to attending an event, my mother taught me this rule at a young age: "Don't go to any party hungry. You never know when they will serve the food, if there will be enough food to go around, or if you will even like the food they're serving." She repeated it so many times that it got stuck in my head, and I continue to live by it today.

There's one problem with the rule though. After a person eats before leaving home, they must then exercise discipline once they are at the event. If the food spread is tempting, it is easy to forget that you've eaten and actually end up overeating. If the appropriate caution is not taken, Mom's rule could lead to weight gain, especially around the holidays.

In general, many Africans have interesting histories and relationships with food. Food represents different things to different people. For example, African families living in villages grew their own food for consumption and to generate income. Depending on the weather and growing conditions, they could have healthy yields that were plentiful, or they could have a small yield and struggle to feed their families. All of this was happening in an environment where ways of preserving food were either impossible or limited.

Another food history is that providing food beyond one's family was rare. Many people did not have enough to feed their own families, let alone friends and neighbors. Therefore, people who could afford to give others food, whether to share regularly or during special events, were usually considered too wealthy or well-off. I remember attending a couple of birthday parties while growing up and being required to have my invitation on hand in case it was needed to prove that I wasn't crashing the party. Most people couldn't afford to throw a party, and those who could had just enough for the intended special guests.

When food was shared with guests, it was always of a better quality than what the family usually had. The best of everything, including food, was reserved for guests. Most Africans believe that if an event did not include dishes better than what they already get at home and in larger quantities, then attending that event is not worth their time and energy. Expectations for event food are very high, which puts hosts under a lot of pressure. They have to ensure that their guests are not only well-fed but also pleased with the food offerings.

Food played a vital role in the success of AWC. Food was used to bring people together and make them feel comfortable and familiar with others and the setting. Of course, that meant having the right type and amount of food expected by the audience. That wasn't always easy to do with women from different countries who favored different foods.

I experimented with different types of foods throughout the years. With the decision to keep meetings short, two to three hours only, my plan was to keep the food light. I thought food that was affordable and mostly snack foods, like chips and dip, crackers and cheese, fruits, etc., was the way to go. I quickly found that my audience expected something quite different than what was being offered.

I learned that whenever the word "African" appears in an event title, people expect African food. If not the authentic African dishes, then at least African "inspired" foods. Depending on the type of event, they may expect every detail Africanized, including food, guests, decor, music, cultural values, language, etc. Unfortunately, not many of the favorite dishes are considered to be healthy or lite. Very often, when African foods are prepared healthier, they don't go over very well with Africans because they don't consider the taste authentic.

The middle of the road were appetizers like meatballs, chicken drummies, skewers, kabobs, sambusas, meat pies, and the like—something small in size but filling. It was also my experience that African women don't care as much for sweets, treats, and desserts. Sweet breads or traditional cakes, which are usually not so sweet, work much better. Some examples are cornbread, rice bread, banana bread, and plain cake.

On the opposite spectrum, authentic African food requires a lot of work to prepare, is very filling, and is quite steep in price. This kind, of course, was the most preferred. However, due to a lack of funding and the challenges of an unpredictable headcount, I had to find creative ways to provide this option.

Get people involved by organizing a potluck: Many African women are raised to be good cooks because of beliefs around traditional gender roles. They are usually proud of their cooking and happy to feed people and show off how well they cook. They are usually open to contributing by bringing a dish to share, which helps to provide a variety of options to choose from.

Work with the restaurant ahead of time to negotiate a flat fee for specific menu items:I was able to work with restaurants to give AWC participants a flat fee for a predetermined menu for an estimated number of people. In this situation, the participants were responsible for paying the fee and made aware of that in advance. However, this only works well if you know for sure you can get the required amount of people to commit to attending the event. Also, it is always wise to have extra money on hand to be ready to make up for no shows. It helps to include language such as "Cancellations less than twenty-four hours prior to the event must be paid in full," when sending out the invitations.

Meet at a restaurant and have people purchase their own food: This is much easier, but it helps to shorten wait time by sharing the menu with participants in advance. Also, alerting management of the number of people you are expecting so that they can be prepared helps things move a bit faster. There were times where the restaurant provided great suggestions regarding specific menu items or helped narrow choices in order to make things affordable.

Collect fee/payment prior to meeting so that food is paid for: This usually works well for catering services that need to have the payment prior to the event. Collecting payment removes the hassle of making out-of-pocket payments or having to track people down.

I always asked about dietary restrictions just because more and more people are experiencing dietary problems. It is also a good way to be inclusive and respectful. I ensured that there were always a couple of nonmeat food items in case anyone needed it. I find that Africans are generally not supportive of nonmeat eaters, so they don't talk about their diets to avoid any unpleasantness. I had a couple of seafood restrictions but not much else. Many Africans enjoy eating spicy foods, but I always requested to have spice as a side item. This way, people could take how much they wantedor pass if they didn't want any.

One thing African women like more than eating great African food is feeding others African food. AWC collected nonperishable African food items for the annual AWC Food Drive. We also provided a meal to a women's shelter as a group volunteer effort, which turned out to be a great group experience.

Rita Jackson Apaloo

From my experience running AWC, I learned that African women really enjoyed and preferred food that they were familiar with. Many of the experiences they had with foods they grew up eating continued to impact their relationships with food. When they got food they expected and enjoyed at events, they felt more comfortable and less distracted networking and connecting with others. And when they had the opportunity, they jumped at the chance to share their tasty cooking with each other.

When it comes to African women and food, the bottom line is to provide food they enjoy and expect, or be ready to hear about it—and not in a quiet or polite way.

Chapter 17

Monitoring and Evaluating Activities

A WC was an experiment of sorts with no manual or examples to follow. It took a lot of trial and error to figure out what worked and what didn't. Creating a plan to operate and engage was smart and helpful. Trying different activities and monitoring and evaluating them helped me learn if things were working as planned. Also, tracking results allowed me to improve the planning process the next go around and hold myself accountable for the things I promised to do.

Collecting data

Had it not been for my program evaluation background and experience, I probably would not have thought to measure results. I knew that in order to measure results, I had to have measurable goals. I had no specific plan in place the first year because I had no idea where things were going. However, I knew that I wanted to get contact information from the women so that I could follow up with them. I also knew that I wanted to get their feedback on the event, and whether or not they would consider attending another one. I also wanted to know what they liked about the event and what suggestions they had to improve. This is how the collection of data began for AWC.

Not all requests for data went over well. I tried a couple of times to collect personal data on things like age, marital status, number of children, household income, and years resided in the United States. The fact that so many were left uncompleted showed that people found those questions to be intrusive. It was evident that they were uncomfortable providing that kind of information, especially to an African-led organization.

Another thing that didn't work was long, exhaustive forms. The event feedback survey form went through several revisions to get the right balance of useful information that could be complete very quickly.

I kept collecting the same information at every meeting and soon I began to see ways to compare the data. For example, the number of people in attendance at each event, the women's countries of origin, and their comments, were all things that I could compare and see patterns.

Managing data

Event data was transferred to an Excel spreadsheet for better management. That means I had to complete data entry shortly after each event. I made a rule to follow up with event attendees forty-eight hours to one week. I preferred forty-eight hours because it was long enough for people to have some reflection and at the same time close enough that their experience was still fresh in their mind. I discovered that at the forty-eight-hour mark, people were more willing to share more feedback about their experience than if the follow up was a week later. People are busy, so by the one week mark, they have moved on to other things.

It was critical to complete the data entry because I needed the information to send follow up emails, which was AWC's preferred form of communication. For those who did not provide an email address (there were some people at that time), I made a point to call them to follow up on their event attendance.

Interpreting results

Results from information gathered and managed were evaluated to provide a picture of what was happening with AWC. Was attendance growing? Were there certain times of the year when attendance was high or low? Is there an explanation for why AWC has a large participation rate among West and East African women versus other regions? How are people learning about AWC? What is the rate of repeats versus one-timers? The data answered a lot of these questions but also left me with many others. I was also able to decide on where to focus my time the most and areas where I needed to devote less time.

AWC data made it possible to share the story of growth and promise to volunteers. Having the skills to monitor and evaluate activities demonstrated valuable leadership abilities. I found that it gave me confidence and comfort that it was possible to make improvements and keep things moving forward.

Reporting and communicating results

I provided ongoing communication with participants, event attendees, and the general public after each event about the number of people in attendance, their comments, and other things. Also, a report was generated at the end of the year that showed combined data from the entire year using attractive and colorful charts and graphs. I received many comments from participants, mostly thanking me for the work being done and encouraging me to keep things going. The reports provided a sense of transparency about what was happening with AWC and reinforced its mission. Was I worried when the trend was not going in the direction I wanted? Absolutely! But I used the opportunity to not only explain why I believed it was the case but also let people know what the plan was to fix that moving forward.

I took a lot of pride in providing information from my monitoring and evaluation efforts to participants. I felt like it was another way to demonstrate that we were in this together. With their help, AWC was growing and changing, and they got a chance to see how they fit in the story while following AWC's progress.

The impact of AWC would not have been possible without having closely monitored and evaluated event activities. Participant information, attendance, and feedback were analyzed. The results were used to inform changes to activities as needed. Findings were put into reports that were shared with participants through various channels of communication and posted online for access to the public. Taking stock and performing ongoing analysis helped to accelerate AWC's progress.

Chapter 18

REACHING OUT FOR SUPPORT

It is always so easy to lose sight of the support from those closest to us. Like the fixtures in our homes that we benefit from but don't think about until there's a malfunction, we tend to take our support system for granted. For example, every time I experience a power outage as a result of severe weather, I become acutely aware of the critical value of utilities to carry out the most mundane functions.

The fact that this is one of the final chapters is evident that those providing moral and emotional support vital to our success are often not given the credit they deserve.

My husband, Jacques, wore many different hats from day one of AWC. He gave his unfailing support throughout and was there when I decided to close shop. This journey would have been almost impossible without his interest, support, and advice.

I am a think out loud kind of person, and fortunately for me, Jacques could listen to me talk for hours at a time. He is a good listener and enjoys critiquing me. All of the conversations kept him up to date on what I was doing with AWC and what he could expect in terms of my availability for scheduled family activities. He was never in the dark about what my desires were and the time and effort it took to implement my plans. I also shared my preparation plans and meeting and event dates with him.

There were so many times I needed his help in order to have a successful event. For example, for one of AWC first meetings, I decided to experiment with proving childcare for attendees. Being the super supportive partner that Jacques is, he hesitatingly but bravely agreed to watch the kids in the lower level of our home while we had our meeting. It didn't work out very well. Nothing disastrous happened, but it was chaotic enough for him to say "no more." After that episode, I tried having volunteers watch the kids, round-robin style, but it didn't go over well either. So apparently, Jacques was not the only one who thought on-site childcare was a bad idea.

Jacques also acted as my sounding board many times. This was critical in helping me look at things from a different point of view, especially an African man's point of view because the culture is patriarchal, and African women are still very accepting of this social system. Jacques gave me insights that I would not have known or even considered in planning and strategizing for AWC.

Jacques and I are both African-born individuals and lived our formative years in West Africa. However, we are from two different countries—he is from Togo, and I am from Liberia. Even more significantly, our lives were as far apart as any could be. He grew up being proud of his ethnic background and cultural heritage. He spoke his native language at home and outside of school and grew up around African ceremonies and rituals, which he respects and values. He is very knowledgeable of African history, people, and its great leaders. Jacques has seen, heard, and experienced things that I find incomprehensible.

I, on the other hand, spent my growing up years in a mining town that was a joint venture of the Liberian Government and American and European entities. The town consisted of expats from Europe, America, and many other countries around the world. The people, neighborhoods, and culture all imitated what you would find somewhere in Europe or America but oddly was situated in Africa. My parents hailed from two different Liberian tribes and were among many African families who found employment in that town. I spoke no African languages growing up, and I learned a watered-down version of African history from school books sent from America and Europe. Where I went to school, books by African authors were limited, and I had no understanding or experience of African traditions and rituals. As a matter of fact, I declared African stories of rituals as myths because I thought they were.

With our backgrounds and perspectives of our African experiences so different, we constantly challenged each other about what was possible with AWC and what was purely delusional. Usually, I was the hopeful one, and he was the skeptic. At the end of the day, I learned a lot from him. I felt safe and secure in sharing my thoughts and plans with him even when they were way off the mark because of my limited knowledge and experience of many things African.

My AWC dream also included defective financial forecasting. That resulted in my having to use family funds more than I could justify. Jacques has a background in finance and was vocal about this, and he constantly reminded me that a lack of funds was not a winning strategy. AWC's accounting was an area of contention between us, even though I knew that he was right. It was frustrating that I couldn't find a solution to fix AWC's finances.

In his recent reflection of our AWC days, Jacques shared that he was impressed with how passionate I was about AWC and later came to appreciate my tenacity and creativity in keeping it going for as long as I did.

My children Rae, Jacques-Philippe, and Alice were also included in my AWC plans and dream. I did my best to share what was going on according to their understanding and interests. Keeping them informed and in the loop made it easier for them to understand my absences when I was busy with AWC. I learned to not only hear their questions and concerns but also find ways to accommodate their requests for their mommy. For example, when they complained about me being gone a lot and wanted to do an activity with me, I took them seriously and made sure to follow through with whatever promises I made.

When AWC was meeting at our home, Jacques took the kids out. On days when they came back before the women left, they were welcome to hang out with us. After all, the ladies were in my children's home, and I felt that it would be cruel to isolate them to a specific area of the house until the "guests left. In fact, one of the reasons I always tried to keep time was so that my kids wouldn't have to stay away from home longer than necessary.

My sisters Joyce and Wokie were also supportive of my AWC dream—as is common for us to support each other in many different ways and endeavors. They were part of the initial group that helped to provide feedback on the mission and vision, assisted financially, and thought through how the group operated in the early months. They continued supporting me throughout the life of AWC. However, similar to my hope for every woman who joined AWC, I wanted their involvement in the long term to be only because they found AWC to be valuable for their personal needs and growth. Joyce and Wokie helped spread the word about AWC with their coworkers and friends in the community, andmany of their referrals became AWC regulars. I will always be grateful to them for all they did to support me in pursuing my dream.

I am thankful and appreciative of the wonderful friends who in the early weeks came onboard and assisted at different levels with supporting and giving feedback on the concept of

AWC. They stuck around long after defining the purpose and mission, which was a tremendous help during the start of something that was so new and different. There are too many of them to list here, but I am thankful and grateful for all that they did to help make AWC successful.

My mother, Nellie, is eternally interested, supportive, and opinionated about whatever I do. Her reaction to my AWC quest was no different. She was always providing encouragement and reminders that such a group was needed and important for women, and she was proud that I was providing the opportunity for the women. Her support meant so much to me, and it helped me to stay motivated.

It was definitely a balancing act paying attention to all the important people and parts of my life while running AWC. Using my planner religiously and compartmentalizing the many different things I had to juggle were two important skills that I intentionally practiced. My planner was critical not only in keeping my meetings and reminders but also for making notes when I met with people, especially AWC participants and prospects. In addition, the planner helped me to remember important family dates and prompts to have conversations with my kids about things they were doing. For example, when I got Wednesday mail from school, I made sure to jot down upcoming activities in my planner to be reminded to get involved or follow up with the kids.

Compartmentalizing was the best way for me to stay present when I was at home, work, AWC, and other places. I can be equally passionate about a number of things at the same time, so it was very important for me to focus on one thing or person at a time. In addition, I was lucky to have ongoing support from family members and friends. Without their help, I could not have accomplished the level of success I achieved with AWC, and more importantly, the experience would have been much less fulfilling.

Chapter 19

REFLECTING AND FINDING MEANING

"A defining condition of being human is that we have to understand the meaning of our experience." — Jack Mezirow

Reflection was somewhat a foreign concept to me during my first years in the United States. I grew up in a culture where it was almost taboo to do the kind of reflection that requires using lessons learned in order to map out a person's future. "God willing" is repeated over and over to indicate that we have no control over our futures and any attempt to do so is blasphemy because God is the author and the finisher of who we are. Unfortunately, this thinking leaves too many sitting on the sidelines and waiting for "God's plan" instead of using their abilities and talents to design their lives. Too often in African communities, making an effort to take stock of one's life and making future plans is seen as trying to take on the role of God, which is believed to bring on bad luck.

I was introduced to self-reflection at business development trainings and in college. I used to have a difficult time with reflections because my brain was never trained to think in that way. The main thing that threw me off was the amount of time that was given to reflect, which was anywhere from a couple of minutes to fifteen minutes. I remembered feeling frustrated and embarrassed as others journaled or shared very insightful narratives after just a couple of minutes, while I came up with nothing. From my perspective, my American colleagues were quickly able to take into account all the content we covered and reflected on how it applied to their lives, learning, or future plans. That was fascinating and awe-inspiring to me!

With an open mind, a fierce desire to learn this new way of thinking, and a lot of practice, I slowly learned how to benefit from self-reflection. It has been a gift. My life has been enhanced by this invaluable skill ten-fold. I've also learned that reflecting with others, as appropriate, provides a multiple effect.

Most of the reflection that was done during my AWC work was in terms of taking stock of what was happening at one or multiple events, and trying to determine what I could learn from or improve about the work. After the work became dormant and I had some time to take a step back and move past the emotional aspects of letting go of the way things were, reflecting on AWC changed significantly. Today, looking back and reflecting on all that transpired has become a moving target because there is just so many ways I can look at it. I drive myself crazy sometimes slicing and dicing all the ways but one thing that is constant is the fact that I would do this all over again if I had the chance. The following are some things that stand out the most as I reflect on my AWC work.

AWC came about at a very interesting time in my life

It had been about a decade since I moved to the United States, I had had some "successes," but I was also feeling somewhat "off." It felt like I was just going through the motions of living, instead of living a purposeful and passionate life. I felt like I was no longer in touch with the real me, who was a vivacious young woman who was creative, bold, funny, hopeful, and determined to impact her world in a positive way.

Looking back now, I think a lot of what I was experiencing was the result of having lived through the civil war in Liberia. Not only had I lived through the war, but I also had been uprooted from everything familiar, had experienced some horrific things, and had been displaced for years. Although I was never assessed or diagnosed by an expert, I am sure what I was experiencing was nothing short of a post-traumatic stress disorder (PTSD). Long story short, it took me about a decade to start recognizing that I was not quite the same person I used to be. The traumatic experiences I had extinguished so much of who I had been. Still, I felt lucky to be alive, healthy, and functioning.

Research shows that when people participate in work and other activities that they enjoy and value, it positively affects their well-being. On the other hand, when they engage in work or activities motivated by things like money, power, necessity, etc., the opposite happens. Their well-being is negatively affected. The difference is internal versus external motivation. Unfortunately, there are too many examples of this phenomenal of aspirations motivated by external forces in immigrant communities. Many in our community appear to be living the American dream—good education, stable employment, homeownership, and the like—yet they are unhappy because of external pressures and motivations.

The prospect of founding AWC was exciting and stimulating for me. I did not hate my job, but I felt like I could be contributing more, especially in ways that utilized more of my knowledge, skills, and interests. AWC was an outlet for me to put all of those things to work. It gave me the opportunity to call the shots, exercise my leadership, be creative without restraints, thinkoutside the box, be valued and rewarded in ways that did not involve money, and just be my true self. Because of my AWC work, I didn't mind doing other work or feeling undervalued in another space. The work provided hope, joy, and purpose.

I was looking for "more"

I was always a "stubborn" child, at least according to my mother. And in the true fashion of "stubbornness," I ignored any hints, suggestions, or commands to pursue work in the medical field. When I graduated from high school, I was set on pursuing a mass communications degree at the University of Liberia. Once I got to the United States, I was told that that would not be possible because of things beyond my control, like discrimination, my foreign accent, and being an immigrant. I didn't know what else I wanted to do, but I knew for sure that I didn't want to enter the medical field. I started off at a vocational school studying to be an office clerk. I figured, if I was not going to be what I wanted to be, at least I could support another person's dream. I learned how to type, file, write letters, enter data at a high speed, and answer calls on a switchboard.

I landed a data entry position after vocational school and was well on my way to achieve my American dream. My employer said I was the best data entry person he (or she) had ever had! I was promoted to lead staff after a short period, then later to a floor supervisor, then a programs specialist, then a fundraising coordinator, and finally an executive assistant—all at the same employer. It was great. I was doing well, making a decent salary, and enjoying working with the team of people there. Yet, I still felt something was missing. I had struggled with the fact that I hadn't earned my degree, so I thought that was the problem. I reenrolled in school, but it didn't fix the problem like I thought.

The bright idea that was AWC

I was fascinated by the African women I met every day, whether at work, school, church, or in the community. It was fascinating to me that these women came from different parts of my country and from different African countries, yet we were able to build friendships around things that we had in common. I also noticed that our friendships were conveniently built around shared activities. For example, at work, we would eat lunch together and talk and laugh but didn't really extend an invitation to meet outside of work, unless for special occasions like a birthday party, wedding, or community celebration.

I also remembered hearing a lot of stereotyping during our conversations, which I too was guilty of. There was a lot of "Liberian women/people are this," and "Nigerian women/people are that." I also remembered thinking that weif would only get to know each other better,we would break down the barriers of stereotypes, and we would have a more united community. That would make people more likely to build relationships across ethnic groups and country lines, I thought. The more I considered this prospect, the more excited I became, so I decided to find a way to make it happen.

Getting it on the road

Because I had always found comfort in the written word, I decided that a newsletter was one way to bring people together, and I wanted to focus on women. Being a full-time employee and part-time student with a family, a newsletter made the most sense to me. I remember writing down a list of questions and being on the hunt for my first person to interview for the newsletter.

My first interview prospect was a business owner from West Africa who managed an African clothing store. I thought she would be great because she provided products and services African women were interested in. It also looked like she was doing well, so people could learn about her success and philosophy around being a successful entrepreneur. Success in America is always a topic of interest to immigrant communities. To say the least, she wasn't excited about my grand idea and was quite suspicious of who I was and what I "really" wanted from her.

Knowing what I know now from my AWC work, it makes sense why she responded in that way. She did not know or trust me. We did not have relationships in common, and I did not take the time to build a trusting foundation. I had limited time and a deadline to meet. She had a business to run and no interest in what I proposed. She was one of a few people who thought I was nuts for asking them to be the subject of a feature story for an audience of African immigrant women.

I also approached a couple of local African community newspapers to pitch the idea of writing a regular column. They were all run by males, and to be fair to them, they did not know or trust me either. They were producing serious news, mostly politics, of what was happening in Africa, the United States, and the local community. They also provided information and resources that people in the community needed and depended on. As far as they were concerned, what I proposed was mostly opinion and entertainment. They didn't think my idea was a great one.

Although I was devastated that my attempts to reach African women through the written word did pan out, it worked for the best. The audience I was going after can read and are highly educated, but they preferred to connect through social interactions and not by reading up on someone. Had I gone that route, it's likely that the format wouldn't have lasted as long as the face-to-face format did. Looking back, I thank my lucky stars for the resistance and obstacles I encountered. They taught me a few things about my audience.

Using what was already available

While wondering where to go next with my idea to bring African women together, my husband and I were also in the process of purchasing our first home. Somehow after the purchase, it dawned on me that I now had a space that I could use to get started. A whole new line of thought opened up to making it a reality.

I wasn't a fan of house parties and neither was my husband. My goal was to plan the meetings in a way that didn't turn into an impromptu party. If you know Africans, you will know that this is a common occurrence. I made sure that there was no music during meetings—another party trigger. This was intentional to encourage networking and connections through conversation. I also made sure to have an agenda with a main topic or speaker, and a start and end time that did not exceed three hours. Although the meetings were being held in my home, I wanted to make sure that there was minimum disruption to my family's routine. It worked because the approach was more professional casual than a social one. I believe that if I had started things off as a social event with music and dancing included, things would have taken a different turn.

The professional casual meeting format on day one set the tone moving forward. Even when the meetings were taken out of my home into the community, the format remained the same.

Money problems

One area where I didn't do so well and kept "sweeping things under the rug," was the financial management of AWC. It was difficult for me to ask the women to make any kind of payment. Because I didn't have disposable income, I assumed that AWC participants didn't have any either. I didn't want to ask anyone for what I couldn't afford.

Knowing that the majority of people in immigrant communities experience social and economic challenges, my desire was to create a space that wouldn't add to the pressures they already face in other areas of their lives. Perhaps providing no costs events in the beginning set a bad precedent for any future earning potential. On the contrary, the idea of a social mixer for African women from different countries and backgrounds was very new and different. I probably would have run a risk had I requested a fee of some kind. In other words, I believed that the women were much more likely to give in to their curiosity of something new that was free than to spend money on the unknown. In the end, a lack of financial planning stalled AWC's work, but I can't see how it could have worked had I introduced any form of payment in the beginning.

AWC created a buzz

One of the things that surprised me was the interest from the larger community when they learned about the uniqueness of AWC—African women from several different countries of origin congregating. I became aware of the stir we were creating when I first started the "Out on the Town" events. While calling around and researching group opportunities, I got questions about the group, and people were really interested in the prospect of having a group of immigrant women becoming a part of their service. Apparently, it was an anomaly for those establishments. Many of them tried finding ways to build ongoing relationship with AWC by offering discounts or adding the group to their mailing list, hoping we would continue to use their service.

I believe AWC could have made a big difference not only by injecting diversity into mainstream establishments but also by providing value to the women through special offers and access to spaces where they did not think they were the target audience.

One of the things about AWC that topped my pride list was my intentional support of African-owned and other small businesses. I also intentionally used community spaces readily available and familiar to the women. Not only did AWC events promote the importance of utilizing community-specific designed spaces but AWC also supported business owners with our presence and dollars. The awareness of the establishments and the group experience using the space often left a positive impression on the women and some of them returned or referred someone after an AWC event.

Capturing AWC

If I could, I would keep everything I own because each one has sentimental value to me. Certain things that people automatically throw out, I keep. Things like receipts, event tickets, magazines, shoes that I don't wear anymore, etc. I do the same with the written word. I am constantly writing things down—usually a couple of different versions of the same thing—clipping articles and quotes that "speak to me," and collecting all kind of books. When I became comfortable enough with reading on a tablet, I started buying e-books and thought that was my saving grace. Not by a long shot. I miss having paper, feeling paper, smelling paper, and taking notes on paper.

So, once I finally accepted and made peace with the fact that AWC was done, at least in its current format, I found myself with years' worth of documentation of AWC from beginning to end. I have a galore of handwritten notes, electronic files, and printed materials. They are all sentimental to me. They are parts of a larger story, including mine and the women's stories. They are part of a story of how I had a dream of and found a way to bring women together in our quests for acceptance and belonging in a place where we don't always feel permitted to be our true selves. Through AWC, we all found understanding, support, and sisterhood.

It was my dream—not theirs

I dreamed up AWC, but AWC needed people to make it a reality. It is possible that I didn't do a good job getting buy in from the women to make AWC more successful and last longer than what it was. Perhaps I could have devoted more time to finding ways to get more women involved in planning and implementing activities. Because I'm largely a thinker and doer, sometimes I don't do a good job explaining coherently what I need from others. Usually, I am often ahead of the person I'm speaking with when I'm conveying a message. Once it becomes clear to me that they have no clue what I'm talking about, I have to switch gears and catch them up so that we are on the same page. Maybe that was the case. I may have thought I was communicating enough through several channels of communication when in fact I was all over the map with my thoughts. The feedback I received demonstrated satisfaction about specific events and experiences, but perhaps they connected those things to the overall goals? I'm not sure.

I later realized that instead of constantly checking in with what they wanted and whether they approved of the AWC events, I could have been a bit more focused on leading with confidence. I admit that I was more confident in the beginning and more worried about AWC's direction in the later years. I was a stronger leader when I was confident and certain of my goals and dreams. The women began to doubt when I switched things up and looked to them to help me shape the future of AWC. Although, that was the idea—bring people together and garner enough input to carve out a newly shared vision. But that did not change the fact that it was indeed my dream and not theirs. The women were prepared to follow but not to take the lead.

Family affair

I once heard about this fascinating story about a couple, and it has stayed with me ever since. I try to retell it every chance I get. I think that it is appropriate for this occasion, so here it goes:

Once upon a time, this couple fell madly in love in high school and then got married soon after graduating. They decided to start a family in the early years of marriage, so the wife got pregnant before earning her college degree. She was happy to stay at home with their child while the husband continued his studies.

The husband was smart, hardworking and charismatic. He did really well in his career, and it was no surprise when he quickly rose up through the ranks and soon became a sought after executive. This status provided the opportunity to travel frequently all over the country and around the world. The wife did some traveling with him in the beginning, but as the number of children grew (four total), she cut back. That meant that many times, she felt like she was raising the kids alone while her husband flew all over the world meeting interesting people, making amazing deals, and fulfilling his wildest dreams. She was happy for him and his achievements and enjoyed the fruit of his labor. She was elated with joy whenever his eyes lit up with each box checked or each goal met.

All this time though, she had a secret. Throughout those years, she envied her husband's life and his successes. She wished she had had even a fraction of the opportunities he had and experienced the high of success and the carefree feeling one must feel when they trust others to take care of the rest as she did for him. She decided to defer her dreams for when the kids were older and didn't need her so much.

Somehow, that didn't happen, so she decided that she would hold off until the kids left home and went away to college. Again, that didn't happen. Then she thought perhaps she would find a way to pursue her longheld dreams when her husband cut back on his travel and work hours. That too wasn't happening.

One day, she felt like she couldn't hold back her frustration of waiting any longer, so in tears, she poured her heart out to her husband.She told him that she loved him even more than the day they first met. She told him how proud of him and his success she was and how she sometimes envied the opportunities he had while she kept things running at home. She confessed that she too wanted some of those things for herself, and she was disappointed and frustrated that he didn't encourage her to follow her dreams, especially after their kids had grown up and left the home.

When she was done pouring her heart out, she looked at him and was confused by the tears running down his cheeks and the deep sadness in his eyes."What's the matter?" she asked.

His replied was not what she expected. "Had I known about your dreams, I would not have hesitated one second to make sure you not only got a fair shot but also my full support. I love you and have always wanted your happiness. I thought you were happy with the way things were."

Can you imagine how the wife must have been feeling in that moment?

I never want to find myself in that situation. AWC's success was largely due to my openness about my passionate for AWC and how important it was to me. There was no question in my household about my commitment to my AWC work. Even my young children knew not only because I told them so often but also because they saw my work. We talked about AWC as a part of something that mommy did and as a part of our family routine. It became so normal for the kids that they often wondered why Daddy wasn't holding meetings for the African men. I am glad I was able to model pursuing one's passion and personal values no matter what.

It is no secret that my husband was not thrilled about my using our household income to finance AWC, especially since we didn't have discretionary funds for miscellaneous use. We often had conversations about this issue, and it wasn't always a harmonious one to say the least. I am grateful that we were always able to find a way to move past our differences in opinion without negatively impacting our marriage.

Here's to you

Thinking back to the years2003 and 2004, I remember how desperate I was to find any information to help me develop my idea, which seemed so daunting at the time—bringing African immigrant women together to create a network. I wished I had somewhere to start, a couple of essays or a person I could ask questions would have been plenty. Without a roadmap, I muddled through and was lucky enough to come away with some experiences that will hopefully help another person who might be looking. Never in my wildest dreams did I think I would have an opportunity to contribute in a minuet way to the history of African immigrant women in Minnesota. I thought it would be a shame not to. So, here's to you, who will do whatever you can to take it a bit further than I could.

Chapter 20

BEING GRATEFUL

In April 2014, I received a community service award: "In recognition of your tireless effort and support to community building and making a difference in the lives of people around you." I was given a couple of minutes to make a remark, and here's what I prepared:

I am humbled by and grateful for this recognition. It means a great deal to me that my African Women Connect work is being recognized. Thank you so much!

AWC provided opportunities for gaining personal development, building relationships for friendship, business, and community, and sharing information. AWC was a big success, and a lot of discoveries were made along the way. Many women expanded their networks by participating in AWC events. Through group volunteer activities, support of local organizations, and creative networking events, AWC saw an increase in interest from the African community in Minnesota and the general public. Because African women consist of individuals who are experts in their own right with formal and informal education, and because their unique experiences can benefit everyone, I was intentional about promoting African women as experts, speakers, and panelists at AWC events whenever possible.

I am definitely proud of the work I did with AWC! Doing AWC work allowed me to do something I'm passionate about—community building and helping to make a positive impact. It was a different kind of opportunity from the job I was being paid to do. AWC work gave me the opportunity to hone my skills in many areas, including program development, management, event planning, and group facilitation. Little did I know that these skills would become useful in career planning and transitioning years later. AWC work, which I never thought of as "work," has opened doors for me that never would have happened otherwise.

It's interesting how something that started simply as a group of girlfriends getting together has now given me a different perspective of who I am and what I am capable of.

I would not be accepting this award today if not for the women who supported me and trusted me to lead them. My family has also been very supportive, including my husband and children, my sisters, and my mother. Without their steady love and support through the highs and lows, and my husband's willingness to let me use our household income to fund my passion, this would have never even been possible. I am grateful for them.

In closing, I would like to urge you to ask yourself these questions if you haven't already: What am I passionate about? What brings me joy and fulfillment? What is the one thing that I strongly believe would make life so much better if someone would just figure it out?

Find out what moves you and then find a way to get it done. Let your planner be your best friend in finding the time even if it's thirty minutes per week. Begin to do something, and you may be surprised where that will lead.

I, for one, had no idea that AWC would take me on a life-changing journey.

Thank you again for this award. It means the world to me.

AWC Unedited Information

AWC Logo Evolution

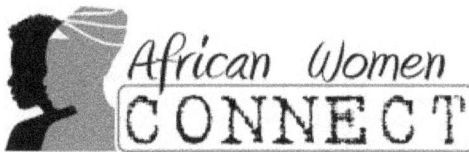

Top: first draft hand-drawn logo image with text

Middle left: first draft silhouette of logo image with text

Middle right: silhouette and text with added element of a crescent

Bottom: current professionally designed logo

Rita Jackson Apaloo

AWC Affirmation©

I accept who I am

I accept the opportunities and challenges unique to me

With courage, faith and determination

I aspire to be the best person I can be

I accept you for who you are

I accept your choice to do what is best for you

Without questions or judgment

I support you in being the best person you can be

I accept you as my sister in spirit

I accept your gifts and your success

United we can overcome fear and negativity

Together we can build a stronger and powerful community

We connect to love

We connect to learn

We connect to succeed

by Rita Jackson Apaloo

AWC Event Attendees Comments

"This was a great event! Great choice of restaurant! Love Tam Tam! Great community of women!"

"Had fun! Nice to meet a diverse group of women."

"Time well spent. Very interesting and informative."

"I think this organization has been long overdue."

"The whole program was really good."

"I have been waiting for a long time to meet women from around Africa in a forum such as this one. I believe we are powerful and if we can work together to empower each other, we can achieve the 'American Dream.' The bonding was phenomenal!"

"I enjoyed the activities and the positive environment."

"Excellent gathering! I loved it and learned a lot about my culture."

"The organizers did a good job getting people together. Great place and pleasant atmosphere. Great group of beautiful women with positive minds."

"Great event. The wealth of expertise and ideas is very rewarding. It's great to see so many great African women."

"For a start, it was a great success. Can't wait to see how this group will evolve."

"Wonderful idea. I believe in the mission and vision of the organization."

"Sitting around the table and dinning with sisters from several African countries gave me a sense of great pride and purpose. The amazing thing is that we all seemed to be like-minded and want to build successful relationships with each other. Very uplifting experience!"

"Thank you so much for such a memorable evening. I was so happy to meet such a group of distinguished women. I believe in AWC's mission and vision and the empowerment of women to affect positive change in each other's lives collectively no matter what the dream. Thank you for implementing what most of us only dream about."

"I found the wealth of expertise and ideas very rewarding! It's great to be among many great African women."

"I enjoyed meeting women of different walks of life, to share ideas and connect with the future.

Sisters Gathering over meal! Splendid!"

"Had a great time meeting many new women from varied backgrounds."

"It was great to see such a diverse group of accomplished African women."

"It feels so good to be surrounded by such kind, intelligent women. I had a fun night; I was not faking it".

"I met new and existing African sisters. The atmosphere was relaxed and inviting to conversations and getting to know the women in attendance."

"It was great to connect with old friends and new people. There was a lot of energy in the room. Great vibe!"

"What is the goal of the group, what are you trying to accomplish by meeting monthly, are your objectives social, political, religious or what? Will The Taste of Africa be your head office?"

"You may want to change up Meeting/Dinner Sites, to keep things fresh! Personally I would prefer us to use new and different locations each time, rather than same location."

"Hmmm maybe some ice breaker games or interactive games that encourage the women to feel free with each other, encourage us all the bond and work together and even help us with name recall. I can help research some games."

"This was great. I like the intro, that everyone spoke and told us who they were. And the food was fantastic."

"The food was great, the location was lacking fresh air and windows."

"From my experience as a journalist navigating the greater MN African community, AWC is unique in its mission and goals. I feel like AWC is very different from most women groups that tend to lean towards cultural perspectives. AWC is definitely needed and should be preserved. Therefore it is important to put "things" into perspective—

numbers, participation levels, concept by-in, etc., and keep plugging away."

"I don't remember how we met, but AWC was so much a part of my life once we did. And I still appreciate it for the friendships and growth AWC afforded me."

"I loved those moments in Minneapolis!"

"I enjoyed networking with you, and the rest of the ladies. I took a lot from there. Keep up the good work!"

Note: Considering that faith and spirituality is of paramount value to African women and event attendees' requests to start events with a word of prayer, Joanna Fuchs' Thankful for Each Other prayer was adapted for this to be inclusive of all faiths. Attendees read out the prayer together at the start of events.

Prayer in its original form. Published with author's permission.

Dear Lord,
As we gather together around this table
laden with your plentiful gifts to us,
we thank You for always providing
what we really need
and for sometimes granting wishes
for things we don't really need.
Today, let us be especially thankful
for each other--for family and friends
who enrich our lives in wonderful ways,
even when they present us with challenges.
Let us join together now
in peaceful, loving fellowship
to celebrate Your love for us
and our love for each other. Amen.

BY JOANNA FUCHS
http://www.poemsource.com/thanksgiving-poems.html

Rita Jackson Apaloo

Prayer adjusted to fit AWC's need.

As we gather together around this table blessed with gifts and good fortune, we are thankful for having the things we really need and those things that we don't really need.

Today, let us be especially thankful for each other--for family and friends who enrich our lives in wonderful ways, even when they present us with challenges.

Let us join together now in peaceful, loving fellowship to celebrate each other.

Note: In 2009, AWC held a Leadership Summit showcasing African Immigrant Women leaders representing different communities. A group of women volunteered their time to organize the event. The summit drew a sizeable crowd and we had a lively discussion on leadership, family, community, and education. We even had male participants who participated in the discussions as well.

Summit Organizing Team
Rita Jackson Apaloo, Wokie C. Freeman, Elizabeth Wayumba, Ama Eli Akakpo Boumi, Elizabeth Rukungu and Gladys Igbo.

African Women **CONNECT**

2009 Community Summit
Leading for Change

DATE:
Saturday, September 26, 2009

TIME:
11:00 a.m. to 3:00 p.m.

VENUE:
Center of Families, 3333 N Fourth Street, Minneapolis, MN 55412

Women face many challenges in leadership positions, including the barriers related to culture and cultural expectations, the choice and/or balance between work and family and the stresses that accompanies positions of leadership. We will discuss these issues with first generation African women immigrant leaders.

PANEL INCLUDES:

Doris Parker, *Liberian Women's Initiative*

Felicia Ravelomanantsoa, *M&I Bank*

Dr. Joyce Onekaba, *Crown Medical Center*

Mariam Mohamed, *McKnight Foundation*

Ngozika Okoye, *Medical Student, University of MN*

PANEL FACILITATOR:

Foriane Robins-Brown, *Nibakure Children's Village*

This event will promote personal and professional leadership as a catalyst for change. There will be food and the opportunity to participate and network. All are welcome.

RSVP: africanwomenconnect@hotmail.com

WELCOME REMARKS

Thank you for coming out to join us for the first African Women Connect Community Summit (though a mini one it is). Our team really enjoyed putting this together and we believe that the topic of women's leadership, from the perspective of first generation African immigrant women is an important and relevant one.

African women have a history of leadership. From stories of ancient queens who led fierce battles against Europeans who came to take over their lands and enslave their people to the remarkable story of ordinary, courageous Liberian women who came together to end a bloody civil war and bring peace to their war-torn country.

Not enough stories of African women as leaders are told. Maybe it is because they are often comfortable leading private lives and leading in quiet and subtle ways. The goal for these women is to get the job done and change lives, preferably without press releases and story pitches.

I guess you can say that African women are finding their voice, if you measure it by western standards. Things are changing—we live in a "show and tell world." We are learning new leadership strategies that are very different from those of our mothers' and grandmothers' time.

Our experience building relationships with African women immigrants in the Twin Cities Metro Area since 2004 African Women Connect (AWC) has revealed that these women are attaining greater levels of success in the American society; the key ingredient of success being personal/professional leadership. That insight led us to plan this event. We've had over 300 event attendees who are natives of an array of African countries and the U.S. (92% African immigrants and 8% Americans).

A recent Star Tribune article featured women in the Somali community and described how these women and many others are ambitious professionals and business owners, contrary to popular belief that African women are passive and submissive. The article mentioned that the trend of African women becoming ambitious professionals and community leaders is "a sign of cultural shift." Many would argue that that is not necessarily the case—but that's not why we're here.

We are here to discuss women leadership with a panel of women who have chosen that path. Women face many challenges in leadership positions, including the barriers related to culture and cultural expectations, the choice and/or balance between work and family and the stresses that accompanies positions of leadership. What's unique about this discussion today is that panelists are all first generation African immigrant women leaders and that's a significant distinction. First generation indicates:

- reinventing oneself/rebranding
- Career change
- support of several households
- no source of support (financial, emotional from those before you)
- raising children in an unfamiliar environment
- and others

The upside is that this country provides tremendous opportunities to reach one's full potential.

3 of many reasons we're having this event today are:
- to celebrate how we're doing as African Women
- to put the topic on the table (issues around women in leadership positions)
- to build on our success

AWC wants to take the approach of building on what's going well.

We are excited to provide this unique opportunity and we hope you'll find your time with us valuable and worthwhile.

Thank You.

Panel discussion notes

Values:

- o Hardwork
- o Believe in yourself
- o Responsibility to family – here and abroad
- o Invest in children – children expected to care for aging parents
- o Don't give up easily
- o Turn what's negative to positive
- o Don't be afraid to dream big
- o You can be whatever you want to be
- o Perseverance is key
- o Have faith (religion, spirituality)

What/who helped you to be where you are today:

- o Talk to people; ask questions
- o Parents made me feel special
- o When you fail, get back up again and keep on going forward

Leadership Style:

- o Open—listen to others; get their input and suggestions; work with others and grow
- o Empower others
- o Collaborate with other
- o Visionary – people look to you for leadership

- o Respect people you're leading

Work/Life Balance:

- o It's a challenge but good for sanity and health
- o I take my kids with me—they're learning from their experiences and by watching me
- o Make time for things that are important to you—be it family or hobbies—keeps me grounded
- o Take time off for yourself
- o Have to make sacrifices
- o It means missing out on a lot at times (including time with kids and family)
- o Take long showers
- o Flexible work if possible
- o When you connect with what makes sense to you, you feel more balanced

African Women misrepresentation:

- o Cultural differences – what's seemed as submissive, we think of as being humble
- o Stereotypes: Somali and Muslim women –double stereotypes
- o We need to remember to represent well in public – how we can combat stereotypes
- o Raise our kids to be assertive
- o Take what's good from our background and culture and what's good from our new-found home

- o Stereotypes hurts when it comes from within own community
- o Younger women need our guidance and leadership
- o We need to stick together
- o We need to educate our men and the general community regarding what we want and how to make it work
- o We're doing good—need to keep on going in that direction

Misc

- o We all have something to share
- o When we come together with common goal, we can do great things
- o Networking is key—we need more of this kind of forums
- o Empower each other—give voice/support each other

Comments from attendees:

- "I enjoyed every moment. Big thanks to our panelists and facilitators. The table discussions were very interesting! I think we could have kept talking if it wasn't for the time keepers :)"
- "African women are hungry for a good forum where they can belong to and share themselves."

- "More awareness and/or advertising can be done to reach out to many women about our existence, events and activities."
- "We should look to partner with bigger organizations for stronger support and exposure."
- "African women who are in solid positions are definitely a bang and we should fish for more - they inspire, encourage and motivate."
- "Please share what transpires in today's meeting and say hello to the rest of the crew."
-

Education Breakout Discussion Notes

Academic Success

- There are three tiers of education in the US: gifted students are a priority, the average ones are on the sidelines and the struggling ones are forgotten. The ones that make it need to be front runners as well as have dedicated parents who are active participants of school activities through funding or donation of time and goods.

- Immigrant children need to get rounded in extracurricular activities (sports, music) to complete their academic experience.

- Private school is a good option to consider if it is affordable as in general their standards related to academics and discipline are higher than the public schools. They also ensure that parents are aware of their children's progress and contribute to their overall learning.

Issues and Challenges

- Children that are born here experience peer pressure and feel the need to "belong" at the expense of their culture and beliefs. It gets difficult to have them focus on school matters and family values.

- Children from mixed families (American and African-born parents) receive mixed messages; one parent might be used to reading to children as part of the routine while the other parent does not consider that important.

- Children are practically raising themselves academically as the majority of parents have no clue what is happening at the school level because of their lack of education or are too busy holding down several jobs to feed the family.
- Children living in poor neighborhoods are particularly disadvantaged when it comes to education because they do not have access to the educational tools that could make them succeed.
- It is a struggle for uneducated parents to help their children succeed; it becomes the mantra "I want you to have what I don't have, but I cannot help you".
- Racism and negative stereotypes contribute in bringing down immigrant children's self-esteem. There seems to be an assumption that if you are black, you spell trouble and you are treated as such.
- There are a lot of immigrant children drop-offs right now because they fall through the cracks. They might have been popular in Africa, but their reality changed upon coming here and they are considered nobodies as they struggle to adjust to the new educational norms.
- The first generation of African immigrant children lacks role models in whose footsteps they can follow.

- Language barriers and culture play a big role in the immigrant children's challenges: what is meaningful in their culture or language might not be in the mainstream's and vice-versa.
- Immigrant children also tend to lose focus or direction when they are coming from a unilateral system that worked for them to be confronted to limitless opportunities in the US.
- The younger generation is living between two worlds and has to fit in both. They do not experience racism the way the first generation did but it is sometimes worse.
- Thanks to the media in the US, it is perceived that schooling in Africa is worthless. This issue is further accented when the traditional k-12 educational system does not work for children that have experienced war and trauma. They get shoved into alternative schools because of the unrealistic expectations that were heaped upon them (inappropriate grade levels, behavior rules, zero tolerance policies, etc).

Parental Involvement
- Parents need to build a strong foundation with their children before they enter kindergarten: they need to be grammar and phonics savvy, know their shapes and colors, etc... They also need to share their knowledge with their community members

and be visible advocates for their children at the school level.

- African parents need to learn child development activities and get involved in their children's learning from the early stages.
- Stay involved; invite your children's educators to lunch, ask about your child's progress and behavior at school, address issues as they come and be proactive.
- Raise awareness with the school system on your children's unique abilities.
- We need to value our African traditions but go beyond them to ensure that our children are successful.
- Parents need to teach resilience and commitment to succeed to their children by showing their example, being there to assist them in their journey and pushing them forward.
- The concept of volunteering as it is understood in the US is foreign to immigrants but it is critical to stay abreast of the happenings at your children's schools.
- Promote open relationships with children and make yourself available to discuss any topic that they put on the table: drugs, "birds and bees", etc. Be leaders with a positive attitude instead of grudgingly following.

Role of School System

- Do not give up on our children!
- The ratio student-teacher is very high (up to 40 children per class); therefore teachers are experiencing commitment fatigue and just getting by with the bright ones.
- Bureaucracy comes in the way of children's progress sometimes: a prime example is related to gifted children whose intellectual capacity is way above the early childhood screening standards but they are considered too immature for entering kindergarten because of their age. One participant had to send her child to Canada to go around this issue as she was not getting any positive results here in the US.

Final Word of Wisdom: Discipline and success start at home with the enforcement of rules and expectations. It is all about finding balance.

African Men's Group –Notes(Living with African women in leadership positions)

AWC: Leadership role can put stress on the marriage; in that case, what works?

- "We have periodic meetings to check in and talk only about family stuff."
- "We need to consciously find time for each other."
- Important to trust that my wife is doing community work and not goofing off and doing other things
- Helps when I (spouse) get involved in some way
- Keeping up-to-date on her activities and progress or to actually get involved in the work myself
- Helps to plan ahead so that I'm not stuck with having to cancel my appointment or having to leave kids unattended
- Communication is key
  - o Keep track of and communicate schedule
  - o Spend time talking about what's happening tomorrow, this week, next week, next month, etc.
- Sometimes you have to ask the critical questions
  - o Is it worth pursuing?
  - o How is it affecting our family's financial health?
  - o How much of your/our time can we afford to commit?

- o "She has to convince me that it's worth it— make the argument; don't expect me to just accept."
- o "There's a perception in the community that the woman who's in the public eye (all the time) is the one in control in the home."
- o The important thing is the bond and understanding between the two people; the strength of their relationship; understanding, accepting and supporting one another's passion, dreams, and aspirations.

AWC: What if the work is not generating income

How do we support the kids not only short term but also long term - saving for college

- How is this affecting our retirement plans or plans for the future (moving us closer or away from plan)
- It takes a special man to support a woman in leadership position.

AWC: How can we put this topic on the table for men to embrace and talk about in the open?

- Bring in a facilitator; subject expert
- Safe environment so men don't feel like their sharing of info will be used against them
- Target specific group of men who are experiencing similar situation; preferably a small group
- Create support group –type environment

AWC: To help with the stress of living with a woman in leadership position (most men don't know how to handle it because they were raised differently and the subject is taboo so they feel isolated in their feelings, thoughts and situation)

- Important to share same spiritual values
- Don't be afraid to talk with trusted source
- Keep fun in the marriage

Men's Group Observations:

I noticed that in the beginning of the session, the men were holding back and not sure how much to participate and get engaged. But as I shared my story, they opened up a bit and share their own experiences as to what they chose to identify within the story I told. As the time went on, they no longer needed my story to put them at ease or point them in a direction. They began to drive the conversation. Having questions and providing examples really helped the conversation get started.

There was a general feeling of relief that the topic was put on the table, especially with other men who were in supporting roles with a spouse/significant other who was a woman in a leadership position. As the men talked and shared their true feelings, other men got that "I know what you're talking about" look in their eyes. Sometimes they even finished each other statements and thoughts. It was a joy to see how they felt more and more at ease with each other as the session went on.

It helped that the facilitator was able to share some of her husband's concerns and objections with the men, who could identified with the stories she related.

The men agreed that they never get the opportunity to share their feelings and concerns with people other than their significant others.

They acknowledged that there are times when family members are involved but usually not in a positive or meaningful way.

AWC Leadership Summit Observations

The 1st AWC summit was greatly successful. I noted several women making new connections during the lunch break. By the time the attendees convened for the round table discussions new friendships had been formed and relationship building was underway. As a time keeper I had the easy time of keeping us all on task and moving the roundtable discussions along. I say I had an easy task because this group of women was very cooperative and time sensitive. They seemed fine with the minimal time allotted to each discussion topic i.e. 15 minutes per topic. I am sure they had a lot to contribute and could have appreciated more time but they adjusted with the tight schedule and did not resist the topic changes even when things got juicy in any particular topic area.

I also noted the desire for the women to know each other more. They were eager to exchange contacts and to get some in-depth knowledge of what new contacts were up to. To me this was a sign of great aptitude and ambition- people want to be aware of things going on.

The facilitators are natural leaders. They were cheerful, positive and inclusive. I remember listening in and hearing one facilitator encouraging a particularly discouraged summit attendant. The facilitator cheerfully reminded the woman that she was so much stronger and had all this wonderful qualities because of her experiences in life- that was so redeeming for the woman- she seemed to light up at that comment.

The women attending the conference were quickly comfortable with each other. In many ways it looked like a discussion among sisters more than strangers. I think the shared immigrant experience of the majority made many in the room feel at home with each other. People seemed to have a great time both during the fun and the deeply touching moments. One woman shared her experience of being searched at the airport for six hours as she was transiting back into the States from a visit to her home country. The other women listened keenly and all exhaled almost in one breath—it was a very sacred moment. No one tried to take away from it; everyone just shook their head knowingly. I think in that space this woman felt able to share because she knew others could understand. I really doubt if she would talk too much about the experience in circles where there would be little appreciation of her reality.

All in all, the summit was a success. I say so because it met a need- it was a bridge for many who don't have friends to make some, it was also a place to make professional contacts. Finally, it was a space to open up and share without prejudice. For next steps I suggest we start by reaching out to those who attended the summit and keep them in the loop. We could also form an online notice board where we can add people's contacts and professions – almost like a resource tool that can aide one in finding a person who provides a certain skill so that we can begin to support each other internally.

AWC Perception Survey

NOTE: In 2011, I conducted AWC's first Perception Survey after noticing the decline in participation in the previous couple of years. I felt like it was time to learn from the community how they perceived AWC's mission, goals and accomplishments. Overall, the results were positive. Finding time to attend meetings was the reason cited the most for limited participation.

AWC Perception Survey 2011 Results

Survey Sponsor and Research Company: AWC

Objectives: to get feedback and perspectives from members, current and past participants, and target audience on organizational mission, vision, programs and services, performance and direction.

Audience description: mostly women of African descent living in the Twin Cities metro area

Sample size: 260 email addresses on AWC listserv of members, current and past participants, prospects and supporters

Dates of data collection: February to March 2011

Response size/rate: 32 or 12 %

Heritage most closely related to:

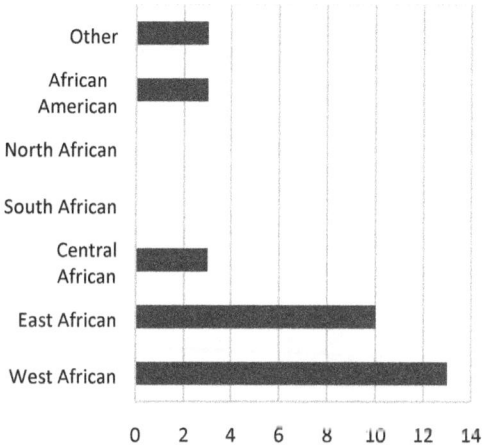

Years lived abroad (US and elsewhere):

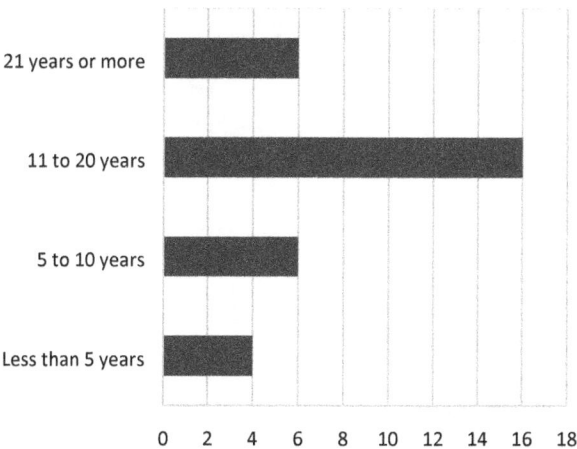

Mission – *to create a network to empower women of African descent,*

linking them to valuable resources and promoting partnerships that strengthen individual and communal success.

Vision – *we envision a world where African women are viewed and recognized as valuable contributors to society by themselves and others.*

AWC Mission and Vision relevant and timely:

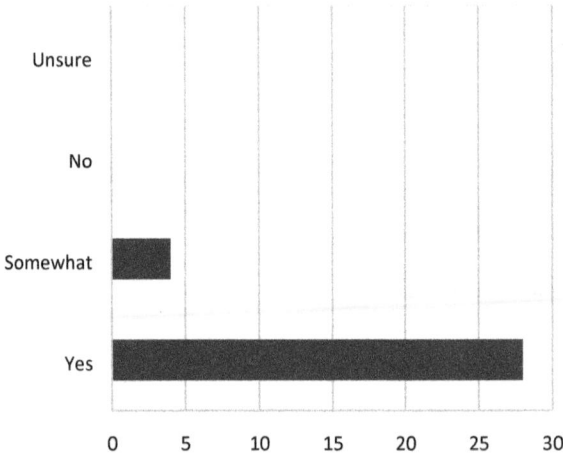

Question 4. Number of times you have participated in AWC events since 2004

Times participated in AWC events:

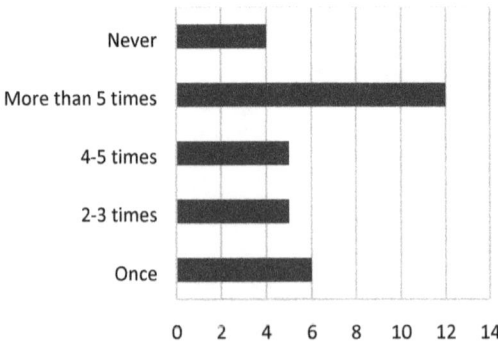

Question 5. Reason(s) why you decided to participate in AWC (check all that apply)

Reasons for AWC participation:

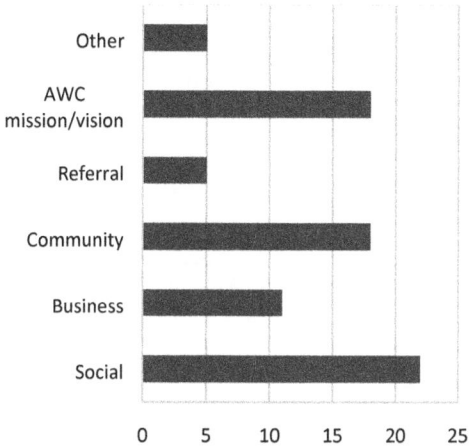

Question 6. How valuable is AWC to you?

How valuable is AWC to you?

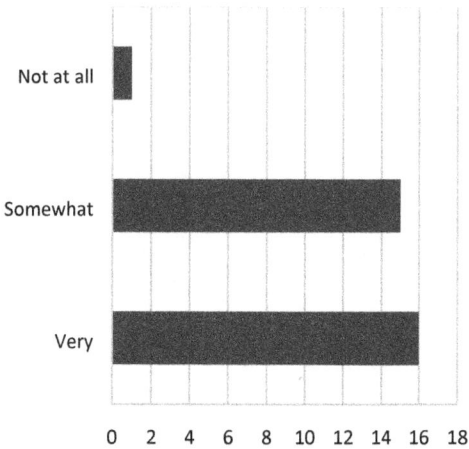

Question 7. In your opinion, what does AWC do well? (check all that apply)

What does AWC do well?

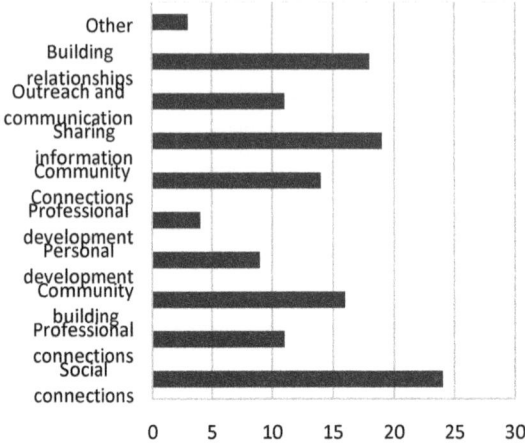

A horizontal bar chart titled "What does AWC do well?" with categories from top to bottom: Other, Building relationships, Outreach and communication, Sharing information, Community Connections, Professional development, Personal development, Community building, Professional connections, Social connections. The horizontal axis ranges from 0 to 30.

Question 8. In your opinion, what areas should AWC focus on? (check all that apply)

Areas AWC should focus on

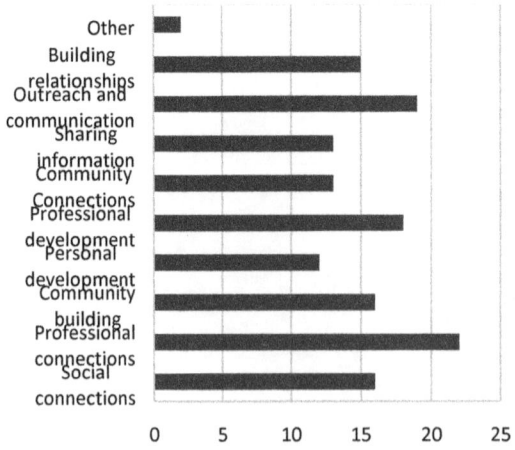

A horizontal bar chart titled "Areas AWC should focus on" with categories from top to bottom: Other, Building relationships, Outreach and communication, Sharing information, Community Connections, Professional development, Personal development, Community building, Professional connections, Social connections. The horizontal axis ranges from 0 to 25.

Question 9. What keeps you from participating more than you currently do?

What keeps you from participating more?

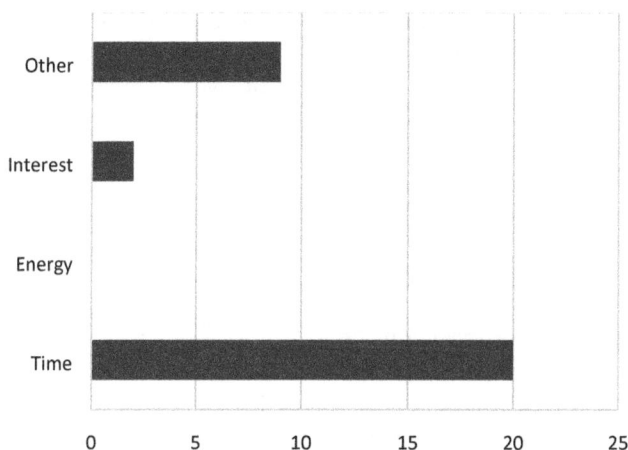

Question 10. What changes would you suggest in order to improve participation and organizational effectiveness?

A. *Time, so far has kept me from participating in AWC. The other factor is that, many times the meeting places have not been convenient, and also the purpose of the meetings has not been clear to me. The biggest challenge for me has been that I do not understand the structure of the AWC. What is the difference between a member and a non-member? What is the purpose of the membership fee? What are the benefits of being a member? What are the fees used for? How can one have a say in the group/organization, etc. It has never been clear to me. Otherwise, I like the concept, but it has never been clear to me where I can fit it.*

B. *Participation - expand outreach to more women through wide advertisement and awareness. Organizational effectiveness - Have a clear organizational structure, with more delegation and involvement of more women who are consistent participants of AWC activities.*

C. *Not really sure*

D. *Location of the meetings; try to find a place where parking won't be a challenge (not always easy but I think people get discouraged if they think parking will be an issue) - Ask people to come up with topics of discussions - Allow people to share information on things they believe can help others. Clearly differentiate marketing and information sharing so there is no confusion and certain people don't feel the objective of the organization are in conflict with their values.*

E. *I believe that AWC is doing a great job and will continue to attract more settled African women compared to new immigrants due the different needs of both. It may be beneficial to target African women professionals and business owners as they may be more open to the networking aspect of belonging to groups and organizations like AWC.*

F. *AWC is already on track for doing that. More opportunities to interact with "power brokers" and professional development workshops would be a plus. Thanks for all that you already do.*

G. *Don't have enough information at this time to make any meaningful suggestions.*

H. *We haven't had any meetings lately. We need to meet a little more often. We are slacking off.*

I. *Try and create more time to be able to participate.*

J. *I'm new to the network through PAWPN Summit committee member.*

K. *Somehow reengage participants from past years. I'm not quite sure how to motivate participants to become members.*

L. *Not sure as my work hours are my biggest reason for not attending. Also, I've been having some problems with the invites, can't open them.*

M. *More visibility. Reach younger population.*

N. *AWC needs other larger organizations' support*

O. *AWC should push towards less elitism so that it can reach more African women.*

P. *I attended one AWC event it was organized with influential women from all walks of life. AWC is a great way for African Americans and African diaspora to connect.*

Q. *Allow participants to present new ideas, information and opportunities to other members. This should include business opportunities and should not be considered marketing.*

R. *Mix some free events in with the paid meetings like a weekend book club that focuses on women issues and interests.*

Email Exchange regarding the survival of AWC

Note: Unedited email exchange with a trusted friend and supporter of AWC about the dwindling numbers and interests of event participants and the path forward.

Friend to Rita – Email #1

I am sorry to hear this Rita I for one feel guilty for not doing more to make this happen.... November is here and we may not have a good vendor turn out .... so understand, but honestly I am more concerned about the board and membership- something is not adding up here and people seem to agree to stuff but don't follow through- to me this may be a sign that they are not buying in but can't say anything... I have spent a lot of time thinking about [the participant's] response that you shared and I must say I agree with her on some level.... My observation so far is that we meet and talk but there is no buy-in hence no motivation to follow through.

I am at a loss really- I find myself wanting to really push AWC and be excited but really holding back because I just wonder if it would be worth the time and effort,... the vision is unique- but the members and board are not buying in..... or is my assessment misplaced?! Oh by the way I am part of the board so I am in the mix too - kind of unsure of what we are about- I mean I have read the vision statement and history severally and want to really push this very unique and out of the box idea.... but here is my concern, is this what these women want? need? or is this just a push in a direction they don't care about- so they agree but are not sold but can't care to say anything......

I find myself wondering if I am deluded or unrealistic and not really understanding the lives of the women who make up AWC. I ask myself- do the women want something that they don't even know how to articulate so they have not bothered to try, or did they just want some simple thing almost like the red hats club- a social club for women to travel, and do stuff together but have no heavy agenda, or is it African women- are we just unable to commit to anything that is not related to nurturing others, or could it be a mix of varied things, or are people just pleasing you and not really saying what they think, what they are concerned about, what they doubt- I am stumped really- what is going on? I'm sure I am naive and don't get it, so please forgive me if I am out of line- I am just trying to understand- what is our psyche.... what do we want- do we even want a membership org?

Sometimes I wonder if people maybe just wanted a forum to meet, make friends, hang out and that's it. There is nothing wrong with that- I mean if it is then all this energy could go to something else Rita- all this energy and resources you put on update e-mails, a newsletter, planning monthly meet up's finding speakers, paying for venues, organizing membership and other meetings, visualizing next steps and implementing them- I mean wow, it is amazing how you have done this year after year- if this was some other business you'd be way on your way to making profits by now.... but this- this is good and big and unique.... but also so dead.

Anyway, just my thoughts- I thought it best not to send it to all just in case I ruffle some feathers and upset people- that is not my intention,.... by the way we are not too good about speaking our minds- it's the African way- we just play along, beat about the bush and never hitting the nail on the head- no one wants to hurt feelings- but if we don't speak up- how will we fix things- how can such a big vision be carried by just one person- you need help Rita- lot's of help.... I think of it this way, Steve Jobs founded Apple, and his buddy Bill gates espoused Microsoft.... but without the ingenuity and energy of scientists from silicon valley and beyond.... these would be just ideas- maybe back yard mum and pop stores somewhere at best..... God gave you a gift- the gift of vision, let's pray for a miracle of helpers... Coz I can't lie to you, I am here but not here- it's like.... what are we doing? Why? who cares? is this worth my time or am I a fool? I am busy and this is one more project- I love it but what do I love about it, what would make me love it enough to really sell it..... do you think the others think the same? Or close? Do you suppose they are lost but can't tell you- they don't want to hurt your feelings- but don't really know what AWC means to them- so they don't sell it!

Friend to Rita – Email #2

You know the one thing I can think of about Africans is the extended family and community responsibilities.... I think of AWC and what it is about- or at least what I understand it to be and then I wonder- do you suppose that for African Women the AWC vision is too progressive and western for them? maybe even unrealistic.... I just got a text from my mum about the passing of a young nephew of mine-one of my cousin's sons... and I am brought back to that place- that place of being an African in America.... with life here but thoughts and responsibilities all over- for me it's literally across 5 continents because my biological brothers are in all sorts of places..... I am sure I am not alone.... A lot of the AWC women have lives here, have children, have community meetings and obligations, extended family stuff, professional responsibility and on and on.... Rita do you suppose these women are stretched thin and can't add yet another thing to their plates and maybe just want a place to relax and bond ? Or do you think they can really carry this vision- is it possibly too daunting- something they want but can't handle because it takes so much work to shape this idea to maturity.... so they stay on the ship to be counted on board but really can't care less if it sinks.... hmmm.... A lot of guessing as you can see- I am just thinking aloud.

Rita to Friend

Wow!

As I read your emails, I must have felt dozens of emotions (if there are that many) at the same time. You probably know by now that I highly value authenticity and straight talk among other things. I always say, with me, what-you-see-is-what-you-get so I really appreciate it when someone dishes that back to me. It is never easy to take but it is always so worth it! I would give just about anything to have 10 or more AWC ladies express themselves the exact way you have---for 5 years I've been waiting for this!

All your questions are valid and none is new to my own line of thoughts or list of questions—from year one of AWC they came up and stayed with me ever since. I was hoping to answer these questions as time went on but there have been very few, if any, answers. I am so aware of them—I go to bed with them on my mind and get up in the morning with them on my mind! In a way, I too have been on a journey and I'm not sure where exactly it's leading but know that I have met some wonderful individuals, have had wonderful insights and experiences and in the end as always, I will have something (junk or value) to sort through and hopefully get me on my next path.

Lately I've been doing a lot of soul searching and recently decided that I don't want to keep going with AWC the way I have for the past 5+ years. But being the committed person I am and knowing that there has always been at least one person who has needed any one of the events at any given time, I always do my best to keep my word and follow through on the dates I set. That being said, I will do my very best to organize the holiday dinner as promised.

2011 will be very different—I'm still figuring it out but I know there won't be any meetings and events (if any, at least not the way they've been). I would like to figure out how to keep the online piece going and perhaps make it a place where African women can go to find people, services, products, events, information and businesses in their local area. Perhaps I will also use it to develop my writing skills as well—I don't know for sure; it's all up in the air.

Everything you've said, my husband has said about 100 times over but I'm stubborn and have to admit that I was selfishly learning things that I needed to figure out on my own. I know that the vision is different and unique for this particular group of women but I needed to try—not just for me but for women like me. I wanted to give us a chance to go down that path and perhaps discover something about ourselves and our community. I know we are not people that spend a lot of time reflecting and shaping the future of our community and people (but we're good about doing that for ourselves and our families). Somehow I was hoping that together we would discover that we could actually do great things together and show the world that it is indeed possible for African women from different countries and background to start from a clean slate and create something unimaginable. That's the dreamer in me—what can I say, I'm a hopeless optimist.

I believe that it's time for that exit plan that I've been avoiding.

I needed to hear all of your questions, thoughts, doubts, feelings, etc. It has saved me more than you know.

Thank you!

AWC Photo Album

Volunteer experience at fundraiser of Nibakure, a
Rwandan orphanage.

Group outing to see Zimbabwean Nora
Chipaumire, choreographer.

AWC Founder, Rita, invited to participate on discussion panel for Eclipsed, Danai Gurira's play.

AWC event hosted at African immigrant-owned restaurant in Minneapolis, 2010.

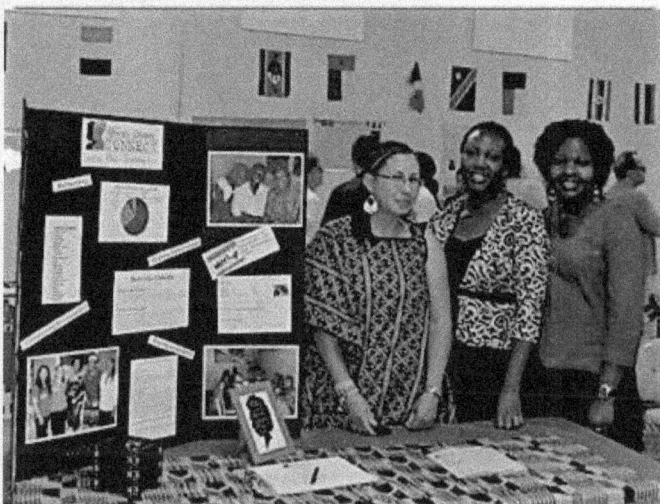

Getting the word out about AWC at a community festival.

Group photo of one of AWC's first meetings.

Holiday boutique vendor at AWC's annual holiday
event.

AWC holiday event at African immigrant-owned
restaurant.

Kids get in the picture after meeting at Rita's home.

Kitu Kizuri Magazine's founder and editor, Angela Ogbolu, brings her message to AWC attendees.

Connecting at an event.

Panelists and moderator at AWC's Leading for Change Summit, 2009.

Facilitator-led conversations at AWC's Leading for Change Summit, 2009.

AWC partnered with various organizations to meetup with Leymah Gbowee, Nobel Peace Laureate.

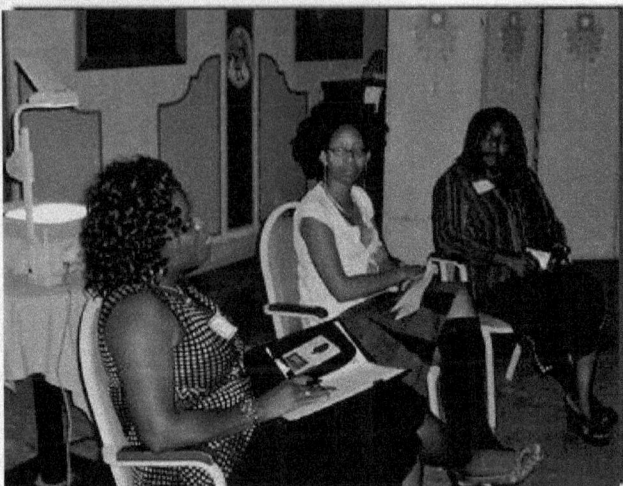

Panel of community leaders discuss working together and supporting one another.

Entertainment showcase at AWC event.

Mshale's founder and editor, Tom Gitaa, posed with attendees after serving as guest speaker.

Group volunteer experience at women's shelter.

About the Author

Rita Jackson Apaloo is passionate about community engagement and issues affecting women and families. She is the founder of African Women Connect (AWC), a one-of-a-kind networking and relationship-building organization for African-bornimmigrant women in Minnesota's Twin Cities metro area. She has a wide range of professional experience in the areas of management, marketing communications, partnership development, program design and evaluation, community education, event planning, and others. Rita has a B.A. degree in Strategic Communications and a Mini Master's in Business Communications. She is also a Certified Professional Project Manager. She has contributed writings to community newspapers such as Mshale and the African News Journal. Ms. Apaloo enjoys spending quality time with family, which includes her husband Jacques, three kids—Rae, Jacques-Philippe and Alice—and relatives and friends. She is a native of Liberia, West Africa.

www.ingramcontent.com/pod-product-compliance
Lightning Source LLC
Chambersburg PA
CBHW021229090426
42740CB00006B/442